# Fast Childcare in Public Preschools

*Fast Childcare in Public Preschools* presents an ethnographic examination of the implementation of fast-policy management models and the efforts of teachers to use these to improve their work organization, and the frictions this brings. Using examples from Swedish public preschools, the book focuses on essential areas of the Lean management model in particular, bringing to life concepts relating to the care and education of children. The book draws on international childcare policy and public reforms, exploring the assignments that preschools are set and argues that separating the pedagogical and the organizational as suggested by proponents of management models is not possible.

This book considers Jamie Peck and Nik Theodore's work on 'fast policy' and 'model power' and analyzes the tensions between the easy-to-use and difficult-to-use in management models. The model form of Lean's management model rendered it difficult to align with existing childcare policy, pedagogical models, and the organization of a preschool. The book explores the utopian dimension of a modern project in pursuit of efficiency and speed in relation to the Lean model and the preschool teachers' work, by asking, 'what are the wider societal implications of the Lean project in preschools?'

*Fast Childcare in Public Preschools* will be of great interest to cultural anthropologists, qualitative sociologists and political scientists, and organizational researchers interested in the anthropology of policy.

**Renita Thedvall** is Associate Professor in Social Anthropology at Stockholm University, Sweden. Her research is based in the field of policy and organizational anthropology, with special focus on the anthropology of bureaucracy and the state. She has explored these issues in various field sites from the EU to preschools. She has a particular interest in meetings, a topic she has investigated together with Jen Sandler through an edited volume, *Meeting Ethnography* (2017, Routledge).

# Fast Childcare in Public Preschools

## The Utopia of Efficiency

Renita Thedvall

LONDON AND NEW YORK

First published 2019
by Routledge
2 Park Square, Milton Park, Abingdon, Oxon OX14 4RN

and by Routledge
52 Vanderbilt Avenue, New York, NY 10017

*Routledge is an imprint of the Taylor & Francis Group, an informa business*

© 2019 Renita Thedvall

The right of Renita Thedvall to be identified as author of this work has been asserted by her in accordance with sections 77 and 78 of the Copyright, Designs and Patents Act 1988.

All rights reserved. No part of this book may be reprinted or reproduced or utilised in any form or by any electronic, mechanical, or other means, now known or hereafter invented, including photocopying and recording, or in any information storage or retrieval system, without permission in writing from the publishers.

*Trademark notice*: Product or corporate names may be trademarks or registered trademarks, and are used only for identification and explanation without intent to infringe.

*British Library Cataloguing-in-Publication Data*
A catalogue record for this book is available from the British Library

*Library of Congress Cataloging-in-Publication Data*
Names: Thedvall, Renita, author.
Title: Fast childcare in public preschools : the utopia of efficiency / Renita Thedvall.
Description: Abingdon, Oxon : New York, NY : Routledge, 2019. | Includes bibliographical references.
Identifiers: LCCN 2018045742 (print) | LCCN 2018058518 (ebook) | ISBN 9781351012836 (E-book) | ISBN 9781138500181 (hbk) | ISBN 9781351012836 (ebk)
Subjects: LCSH: Education, Preschool—Sweden. | Preschool children—Sweden. | Child care services—Sweden.
Classification: LCC LB1140.25.S8 (ebook) | LCC LB1140.25.S8 T43 2019 (print) | DDC 372.2109485—dc23

ISBN: 978-1-138-50018-1 (hbk)
ISBN: 978-1-351-01283-6 (ebk)

Typeset in Bembo
by Apex CoVantage, LLC

For my son, Valde

# Contents

*Acknowledgements*   x

1 **Introduction: the Lean management model in preschools**   1

*Immutable translations of fast policy 3*
*Neoliberal politics in Swedish childcare policy 5*
*Rolling out the red carpet for Lean 9*
*Meeting ethnography in and the everyday activities of preschools 10*
*Outline of the book 15*
*References 17*

2 **Words: the policy words of preschools and management models**   21

*Moveable words with a thing-ified quality 23*
*Lean policy words in the automotive factory 24*
*Policy words in the world of preschools 27*
*Working through policy words among preschool children 30*
   *Gender equality in the everyday experiences of preschools 30*
   *Individuality in co-operation 33*
*Moving Lean policy words into Swedish public preschools 34*
*Conclusion: in the name of efficiency 38*
*References 39*

3 **Meetings: Lean meetings and preschool circle time**   43

*Meetings as events-that-model 44*
*The meetings of management models 46*
*Making good, democratic citizens during circle time 47*
*Working through pedagogical reflection meetings 50*

*Turning an information board into a Lean board 56*
*Conclusion: in the name of improvement 61*
*References 62*

## 4   Colour: colours at work in play and in management     64

*Colours as transformative and provoking responses 65*
*Putting Lean colours to work 68*
*Colours as play and pedagogy in preschool 69*
*An aesthetics of evaluation 72*
*A medium of transformation 75*
*Visualizing the successes and failures of Lean 79*
*Conclusion: Lean colours as a political force 80*
*References 81*

## 5   Flow: eliminating waste along the assembly line     83

*Smoothing machines and efficient flows 84*
*The flow of Lean 86*
*Assembling in the yard to move into the preschool 87*
*Learning how to complete a value-stream mapping 89*
*A value-stream mapping at Caterpillar Preschool 92*
*Conclusion: the Lean smoothing machine 96*
*References 97*

## 6   Plan: hoping for an efficient future     98

*Plans and the hope for a better future 100*
*Action plans and PDCA cycles 102*
*Planning occurring on the fly 102*
*Trying to turn Lean plans into action I 106*
*Trying to turn Lean plans into action II 109*
*Trying to turn Lean plans into action III 111*
*Conclusion: the agentic and affective powers of plans 115*
*References 115*

## 7   Conclusion: the utopia of efficiency     117

*Model frictions 118*
*Model utopia 121*
*Model acceleration 122*
*Model power 124*

*Model failure  125*
*References  128*

*About the author* 130
*Index* 131

# Acknowledgements

A book is never written by the author alone, especially not an academic book that obtained its research material through fieldwork among people. I would like to start by extending my sincere gratitude towards the preschool teachers, the Lean coaches, and the municipal administrators who welcomed me to conduct my fieldwork among them. It might not have been the book they or I envisioned when I began this project, but it would certainly not have been possible to write it without their generosity in opening up their workplace. Working with people who make it their job to care for and teach young children has also taught me the utmost respect for and importance of the profession of preschool teacher.

I would also like to thank my colleagues at both Score (Stockholm Centre for Organizational Research) and the Department of Social Anthropology at Stockholm University who have shared their insights at research seminars or in conversations, for their input has improved this book substantially. I would especially like to thank Kristina Tamm Hallström who, in the beginning of this project, supported my work both financially and through research collaboration. Our work laid the groundwork for the Words chapter in this book. I am also extremely grateful to Score's two guest researchers, Gustav Peebles and Cris Shore, whose insights improved my thinking and contributed greatly to the final product as I was finishing my manuscript during the spring of 2018.

I have also received moral and scholastic support along the way. Helen Schwartzman read an early version of the book and made extremely helpful suggestions. Along with the other participants at our meeting panel at the EASA (European Association of Social Anthropology) in 2016, she helped me sharpen my Meetings chapter, as did my 'meeting ethnography' collaborator Jen Sandler. Hege Høyer Leivestad and the participants, especially our discussant Krisztina Fehérváry, in our colour panel at the AAA (American Anthropological Association) in 2016 helped me advance my thinking in regards to the Colour chapter. Torbjörn Friberg read an early version of the Words chapter and prodded me to dig deeper, which was very valuable. The members of Score's Scientific Advisory Board advised on the Plan chapter – especially Sue Wright, who alerted me to think about 'Lean time'.

And finally, I would like to thank the Swedish Research Council and the Riksbankens Jubileumsfond, The Swedish Foundation for Humanities and Social Science, whose financial support for this project has been invaluable. I would also like to send my sincere gratitude to Nina Colwill for helping me to turn my Swenglish into English and for making valuable suggestions that made my wording sharper.

Finally, I would like to send hugs and kisses to my son, Valde, to whom I dedicate this book. Without you, this book would never have been.

# Chapter 1

# Introduction
## The Lean management model in preschools

Unit Head Greta, who was responsible for the preschool, had just announced that the four preschools in the unit would start working with Lean. At first I couldn't understand what she was talking about. I thought she had said *lin*, the Swedish word for 'flax', which is pronounced the same as the English 'Lean'. My head spun, and I made a quick association to *linne*, the Swedish word for 'linen', thinking that they might have been planning to do something with fabric. Not that that made much more sense, but at the time it was the most reasonable thing I could imagine. When she explained that Lean is a management model that originated in the automotive industry, I knew immediately what she was talking about. A few years earlier I had been involved in an EU project about the automotive industry in Sweden, and had encountered the Lean management model in the course of our research (Garsten et al. 2006). But this time I was attending a Preschool Council meeting of my son's preschool in my role as a parent.

Thoughts began racing through my mind. What did I know about Lean? I knew that it involved working in teams to make continuous improvements in the work process, to make the assembly line run more efficiently, all the way to the customer. Lean was about eliminating waste in the production flow. I knew that it involved daily meetings in front of a whiteboard to go through what had been working and what had not been working over the past 24 hours. I knew that the Swedish truck company, Scania, used green, yellow, and red lights on a board erected in the factory, and that green meant they were in line with the target set for the number of trucks that should be produced that day, yellow meant that they were falling behind, and red meant that they were seriously behind. I knew that Lean included a whole range of values and tools related to efficiency: waste elimination, flows, and continuous improvements. What a strange idea to bring that management model into preschools. Where is the flow and where is the assembly line in a preschool? What can be made more efficient in preschools? What targets could be measured with green, yellow, and red? I realized that I needed to study this strange introduction of Lean in preschools as a researcher.

And strange it became. This is an ethnography of a failure, why an organizational reform using a management model from the automotive industry couldn't help but fail in preschools. It was a failure in recognizing that the context in which the Lean management model landed was so fundamentally different from the context in which it began that it could not possibly be useful. The notion of failure is, of course, a relative concept. I am focusing on failure in the sense that the Lean management model was used in preschools with the intention of making the preschools' organization into a Lean organization – that the staff members would work through Lean and use Lean management tools to organize their work as part of their everyday preschool activities. Failing schemes come as no surprise to anthropologists and social scientists with an interest in development and planning (Abram and Weszkalnys 2013; Ferguson 1990; Latour 1996; Li 2007; Scott 1998). A management model works in a way similar to many development schemes that introduce something that originated in one organization with the goal of restructuring another organization. This scheme came in the form of a management model – the Lean model – a model that was difficult to align with existing childcare policy, pedagogical models, and the organization of a preschool. So Lean ended up operating as a model that had been bolted on to all the preschool activities that staff was already required to handle. Nonetheless, even as an appendage, Lean was able to suggest practices and interventions that were previously foreign to the preschool world and make them thinkable (cf. Ferguson 1990; Li 2007). This book is about the non-translatability of management models and the model form. And it is about what the Lean management model *did* accomplish in Swedish public preschools, which occurred even as the model was failing.

The idea that a management model from the automotive industry could be easily applied to children in a preschool defies common sense in many respects. Yet there are consultants, university professors, management books, and management model handbooks that convincingly argue otherwise, capitalizing on the promise of delivering a rational, efficient, Lean organization (Liker 2004; Modig and Åhlström 2012; Womack et al. 1990; Womack and Jones 1996). By making these promises, management models like Lean have 'model power' (Peck and Theodore 2015b), with the ability to be rapidly diffused and enthusiastically promoted by expert networks. Management models arrive as packages and are, by construction, designed to bring a new, better way of organizing work. As Peck and Theodore (2015b) have noted, the very word 'model' signals reconstruction on another site. It suggests something that would magically align with the context in which it is placed. Management models come with the idea that any organization can adapt to it. Management models work as 'immutable mobiles', then (Latour 1986, 1987), in the sense of a form that includes specific ideas, language, technologies, and actors (actants) that can be seen to be abstracted and transported to serve similar purposes in another domain. Thus management models become 'fast policy' (Peck and Theodore 2015a), easily moved across the globe, promising a ready-made solution, often stamped 'best practice'. Lean is a specialized, relatively closed immutable system with a high degree of autonomy that landed in a preschool environment promising leaner, faster, more efficient childcare.

My thesis here is that the 'model power' of fast-policy management models, easily transported into new domains, makes them both easy and difficult to fit into the practical realities of these new domains. It is the tension between the easy to use and the difficult to use in management models that are explored in this book. I ask four questions: What type of dispositions does the Lean management model entail? How are the frictions played out between what the model can accomplish and what the preschool world needs? How do preschool teachers enact the notion of efficiency inherent in the model? And what societal implications does it have? In doing so, I develop an ethnographic account of Swedish public preschools and the preschool teachers' efforts and struggles to make sense of and use the Lean management model to improve their work organization, while exploring the frictions these efforts engendered. To emphasize how Lean has been bolted onto preschool activities, I have included not only the preschool teachers' attempts to use Lean, their own established working practices and organization of work, but also the everyday activities of preschool teachers and children, to shed some light on the reasons why Lean was doomed to failure and why management models do not transfer as easily into new contexts as their sellers would have people believe. Theoretically, I understand Lean and other types of policies guiding and organizing preschool activities as actors or actants (Latour 1987). I follow the work of Shore and Wright (1997, 2011), who describe policies as having agency in the way that they shift action, perform tasks, and endow certain knowledge and competences. I focus on what Lean as a management model does in the world, particularly in preschools.

## Immutable translations of fast policy

Fast-moving management models like Lean, which are entering organizations all over the world, can be seen as a classic anthropological story of cultural diffusion – or perhaps better still, of translation. The notion of translation here points to the 'same-yet-different' (Gal 2015) logic: To make sense in the new context, ideas and modes of being must adapt and be incorporable into the modes of being/practices and ideas of the new context (Urban 2001). Only then can they undergo a rebirth, including these new manifestations and elements forming new expressions. This perspective echoes the anthropological literature on globalization, particularly concepts such as 'hybridization' and 'creolization', which help to explain how the context in which new ways of being are incorporated affect the way these new ideas and modes are understood and acted upon (Appadurai 1996; Hannerz 1992, 1996). We see in management models how ideas and modes of being, behaving, and understanding are spread around the world and translated into new contexts. In organization theory, this translating process is referred to as 'editing' (Sahlin-Andersson

1996), indicating that it relates to the way a management model is interpreted in the scripts and discourses of manuals specific to the organizational context. As Urban put it, 'the original is dead (or maybe it is not), but the original lives on in its copies' (2001: 2).

The ability to amend, edit, or translate partly explains the survival of management models as they move into new contexts. Drawing on Latour's (1986) concept of 'immutable mobile', however, I argue that it is possible to translate management models only to a minor degree and only within the framework of the models. Latour (1986) refers to immutability as translation without corruption. He focuses primarily on inscriptions, a key feature of which is their ability to attain identical duplication. Latour moves in the world of laboratories and scientists and argues that it is through the inscriptions in lists, files, graph papers, and maps and by making a subject flat that scientists are able to master and dominate a subject. It is the flat surface that enables mastery, as it becomes reproducible and possible to reshuffle and recombine, while maintaining optical consistency (Latour 1986). As Latour proposes, 'the best of these mobiles had to do with written, numbered or optically consistent paper surfaces' (Latour 1986: 21). They are stabilized, and that stabilization affects what they can do in the world. It is the stabilized form of the model that sets the focus on certain ideas, values, and practices rather than others.

In this way, management models work as an example of what Clifford Geertz (1973) termed a 'model for' organizations rather than a 'model of', which would focus instead on the way the organization works, and from this vantage point develop a model out of its physical relationships, activities, people, and objects. It is the 'model for' form that makes the Lean management model difficult to align with other elements of the childcare policy assemblage, because it comes with ready-made values, language, templates, and tools. These are adjustable in some ways, as can be seen when the Lean management model moves from the automotive industry into childcare, albeit only to a minor degree, as it retains the model's language, templates, tools, and overarching values. The success of fast-policy management models moving across the globe cannot then be attributed to their easy adaptation to new contexts. Part of the answer to their almost epidemic diffusion and mobility is to be found in their immutability and commodification. Through their immutable commodification, management models like Lean move as inscriptions in management books, PowerPoint presentations, and other promotions of the model, through the help of Lean consultants, or Lean coaches, linking places and professions and exercising power over organizations far separated in space and time. Another part of the answer to fast-moving management models lies in an understanding of management models as organizational fashions, travelling around the world (Czarniawska and Sevón 1996; Røvik 2000; Sahlin-Andersson and Engwall 2002). This can also explain the fast-changing, travelling understanding of which management models work and which do not work at any given time. There is something particularly appealing about newness and the promise of efficiency in the modern era of 'social acceleration' (Rosa 2013). I return to this notion in the concluding chapter.

## Neoliberal politics in Swedish childcare policy

Sweden is associated with a strong state; strong unions; a goal of full employment; high social insurance entitlement levels; and public funding of hospitals, education, eldercare, and other strong social services. Historically, these social democratic ambitions were articulated in the 'Swedish model', in which social security was seen as a precondition for economic development. The community tended to accept economic change – being forced to move in order to find work or re-educating themselves when jobs disappeared. The social security that employees enjoyed while pursuing new avenues for work was thought to be the basis for their acceptance. If people lost their jobs due to a restructuring of the economy or the labour market, they should be protected through social security. The goal of full employment in Sweden in the 1970s and 1980s was made possible partly because the public sector hired more employees. The public sector also played a social role in employing people who would currently be regarded as 'unemployable'. The idea of childcare being provided by the state was part of the endeavour for full employment and high levels of social services.

At the end of the 1960s and the beginning of the 1970s, when many women entered the labour market, there was an increased need for childcare. In 1968, the government launched an investigation to generate a proposal for solving the serious shortage of childcare services in Sweden. The outcome of this investigation, which was wrapped up in 1972, laid the groundwork for the 1975 Act regarding preschools (SFS 1973:1205).

Under the Act, municipalities were given the responsibility of offering preschool activities to all six-year-olds. This was not enough for working parents, however, and a famous slogan from the protesting parents of the 1970s was: *Ropen ska skalla – daghem åt alla* (Shout it loud and clear – preschool for all – although the English translation lacks the same rhyming factor as the Swedish). During the 1970s and 1980s there was a vast expansion of preschools, mostly run by the municipality and subsidized by the taxpayer. In 1995, it was also stipulated that working parents had the right, by law, to tax-financed childcare if needed. In 2000, this right was extended to the unemployed and to parents on parental leave, giving them the right to have their children in preschool for at least 3 hours a day or 15 hours a week.

In comparison, the public demand for childcare expanded in England in the 1980s and the day nurseries nearly doubled between 1989 and 1994, provided primarily by private, for-profit organizations (Moss 2012). Since 1998, the English system has also provided nursery schools for children from three to five funded by state grants, if they meet the conditions of the National Curriculum – the Statutory Framework for the Early Years

Foundation Stage[1] (James 2012; Moss 2012). Compared to nursery schools, the day nurseries are for children from birth to five years of age, and whether private or public, are paid for by the parents. The French system also provides free preschool – *école maternelle* – from the age of three (or two in some areas) until the age of five, integrating preschools into the education system with an emphasis on education (Neuman 2009). The English nursery schools, as the name suggests, focus on early education, whereas the day nurseries focus on childcare (James 2012). Thus England and France make sharper distinctions between early childhood education and childcare than Swedish preschool do. In the Swedish system, care and education are integrated throughout the preschool years from around the age of one until the child moves into the regular school system at the age of six.

Although there is no legal requirement to have children in preschools as there is to have them in school, the Swedish state has provided incentives to encourage parents by stipulating that preschools in Sweden are free of charge for children from the age of three, for 3 hours a day or 15 hours a week or 525 hours a year. Parents whose children attend preschool full-time or for more than 15 hours a week (which applies to most parents in Sweden) pay a subsidized fee for the remaining hours, based on family income. A maximum tariff,[2] introduced in 2002, is still in place. Currently, there is a general view, backed by the Swedish state, that all parents should be able to afford to put their child in a preschool if they want to, and about 80 per cent of all children enter childcare services between 12 and 18 months of age.[3]

All Swedish preschools are governed by the *Curriculum for the Preschool* (2011) (hereafter called Preschool Curriculum or Curriculum) and the Education Act (SFS 2010:800). It was not evident that preschools should be considered schools with their own curriculum. In 1980, the Act regarding preschools was abolished, and childcare was incorporated into the Social Services Act (SFS 1980:620), signalling a view of childcare as care rather than education. It was not until 1997 that stipulations about childcare were moved from the Social

---

1 I present the Statutory Framework in Chapter 2.
2 If the monthly household income in 2018 is greater than 46,080 SEK (~ 4,680 EUR; 5,275 USD), the parents pay the maximum fee, which, for a child between one and two years is 1,383 SEK (~ 138 EUR; 158 USD), and for a child between three and five is 922 SEK (~ 92 EUR; 105 USD).
3 In the Swedish social insurance system, children's caregivers are economically compensated for 195 days for each parent if they take parental leave from work. (Parental leave is also available to non-parent caregivers.) In 2018, caregivers receive almost 80 per cent of their salary up to a maximum of 37,919 SEK (~ 3,792 EUR; ~ 4,339 USD) a month to each parent. Parental leave is paid by the day, so parents can choose how many days a week they want to receive the funding, thereby prolonging the time they are on parental leave. There is cap of 967 SEK per day (~ 96.7 EUR; ~ 110 USD), which means that the compensation can reach only some 80 per cent if the caregiver earns the maximum. Caregivers can extend their parental leave for an extra 45 days each at the minimum level of 180 SEK a day (~ 18 EUR; ~ 21 USD). Parents can divide the days between them by transferring days to each other, but 90 days at the higher benefit level are reserved for each parent and cannot be transferred.

Services Act into their own chapter in the Education Act (SFS 1997:1212), and in 1998 preschools were given their first curriculum. In 2010, the Education Act was changed to place even greater emphasis on the pedagogical and educational mission of preschools. It was also stipulated in the Act that municipalities must offer preschool free of charge from the age of three, but with the same time restrictions as before: 3 hours a day or 15 hours a week or 525 hours a year.

This development signalled a view of preschools not merely as places for childcare, but as schools, as places of education that should be open to all children from the age of three. This position was further emphasized by the *Reggio-Emilia pedagogy*,[4] which was imported from Italy, and many, if not most, public preschools in Sweden were inspired by that pedagogy. Reggio Emilia underlined the fact that children are in a constant state of learning and that preschools should offer a searching, project-planning practice with experiments, interpretation, and reflection; Reggio Emilia considers group learning the highest form of individual learning (Wurm 2005). Reggio Emilia underscored the importance of taking advantage of children's will to create and examine in relation to the preschool environment, teaching and learning through relationships, and documentation as an integrated process (Edwards et al. 2012). I return to the Preschool Curriculum and the Reggio-Emilia pedagogy in Chapter 2.

The Swedish welfare state has not been immune to neoliberal politics and global market ideals and there have been changes during the last decades. Full employment is no longer an ideal, and mass unemployment has become a reality. Social insurance entitlement levels and services have been reduced and subjected to increasing sanctions. Market-based solutions have influenced the welfare state politics of Sweden and have gained a stronghold as an organizing principle and ideal model for social life. The very idea of what social security means has shifted towards more of a 'makeshift ideology' (Garsten et al. 2015). During the 1990s, when ideals of outsourcing and efficiency through competition gained ground, the public sector came to be seen as a private corporation that needed to be efficient, not to 'waste' taxpayers' money on services and people who were not strictly connected to the core activities of the public sector. Many in-house activities, such as cleaning of public buildings, were outsourced to private companies that were engaged through processes of public procurement.

Even as the market logic works as a guiding principle for welfare state politics, it is also permeated by a bureaucratic logic whereby work practices should be as efficient as possible and tasks and people in the labour market are

---

4 The Reggio-Emilia pedagogy, originally from the Reggio Emilia region in Italy, was imported to Sweden in 1992 when the Reggio Emilia Institute in Stockholm was founded. One of the founders was Harold Göthson, who worked for the Swedish government developing the first official curriculum for Swedish preschools and leisure-time education in the 1980s.

classified and made measurable in order to demonstrate performance – a logic understood by scholars as the bureaucratic heart of neoliberalism (Power 1997; Rose and Miller 1992; Shore and Wright 2000). A useful concept pertaining to these processes is the notion of 'management bureaucracy', which Hall (2008) describes as a way of capturing market and client ideals with increased bureaucratization and the advancement of the 'audit society' (Power 1997). Anthropological work on the rise of 'audit culture(s)' (Shore and Wright 2000, 2015; Strathern 2000) has shown how work practices in public organizations are increasingly dominated by the management techniques of New Public Management (NPM) (Hood 1991; Sahlin-Andersson 2001; Shore and Wright 2000), of which Lean is a prime example. Lean management was one of several policies and tools governing and managing preschools. In fact, municipalities had a high degree of independence, and not all Swedish municipalities chose to use Lean. Other municipalities used result-based management (RBM), for example, to manage the public welfare services, including preschools.

Peck and Theodore (2015a) suggest that it is an oversimplification to argue that global policy models serve as a support system for neoliberalism; rather these processes work in tandem (cf. Bear and Mathur 2015). In recent decades, the Swedish public sector has also become a laboratory for testing different private-sector management techniques and expanding knowledge particular to management models (Sahlin-Andersson and Engwall 2002). Public organizations have come to be seen as organizations in need of management in order to be more efficient and offer quality public services (Brunsson and Sahlin-Andersson 2000; Strang and Meyer 1993). Since the scientific management movement at the beginning of the 20th century, there have been numerous attempts to control and manage people, discourses, and practices in organizations through various management techniques. There is a whole genre of management books, bestsellers with catchy slogans and titles, connected to people described as management gurus (Huczynski 1993). Peter Drucker's (1954) notion of management by objective, Tom Peters's search for excellence (e.g. Peters and Waterman 1982), and Peter Senge's (1994) idea of the learning organization are but three examples. Lean management (Womack et al. 1990) is yet another, created within the automotive industry and now used in both the private and public sectors to manage and govern work processes and employees.

But even though the Swedish public sector's organizational landscape is different today, the taxpayer still funds social-welfare systems, including preschools. In the current preschool system, each child holds a tax-financed voucher – a pot of money – that can be used at the public or private preschool of the parents' choice. This has opened up a number of private initiatives providing childcare, from personnel-run co-operatives to high-risk capitalist conglomerates. It is a neoliberal preschool market created in the name of free choice, but with some of the still-recognizable features of the Swedish model, in which the state subsidizes preschool fees so that most, if not all, parents can afford to put their children in preschool. Thus the preschool system exemplifies a Swedish version of neoliberalism, where almost all Swedish preschools are public and heavily subsidized by the taxpayer. In order to create free choice, however, some preschools are run by private companies and others by municipalities. This book focuses exclusively on municipal preschools, in an effort to document their response to these new conditions.

## Rolling out the red carpet for Lean

The idea of market-based solutions and free choice working hand in hand with ideas of efficiently run public organizations and audit culture may make the idea of introducing Lean in Swedish public preschools more understandable. The conditions in the preschools where I did fieldwork were another reason why it could make sense to the heads of preschool units and preschool teachers to introduce a management model from the automotive industry.

In the metropolitan-area preschools where I conducted my fieldwork, there was a shortage of educated preschool teachers, a lack of preschool facilities, and many children requiring preschool placement. The ratio of teachers to children has essentially remained unchanged at 5.2 children per teacher between 1995 and 2015.[5] Over these two decades, however, the tasks required of preschools have become more complicated, and include greater pedagogical responsibility for the teachers. The Preschool Curriculum had introduced new pedagogical assignments and a need to plan and reflect on these activities in new ways. The teachers had several planning hours per week included in their work time, which meant that there were actually fewer staff members in the group with the children than appeared on paper. Furthermore, at least one staff member, often two or three were usually off sick, home with their own sick children,[6] absent for training, or in a meeting, and there was not always room in the budget for substitutes. And staff members were not easily replaced by substitutes, especially on pedagogical assignments.

In this working environment, the preschool teachers hoped that Lean would deliver what it promised: a more effective organization of the workday to provide them with more time with the children. As a staff member doing participant observation in preschools, caring for and teaching the children, I saw how the plans drawn up in the weekly meeting or other meetings played out or did not play out in the preschool environment. Executing the plans was a complicated task, as they were often based on the assumption that the entire staff was

---

5 www.jmftal.artisan.se/databas.aspx?presel#tab-0 (accessed June 2018). Data provided by Swedish National Agency for Education

6 In the Swedish social insurance system, children's caregivers are compensated if they miss work because they need to be home with a sick child. This service is called 'temporary parental leave' and is based on the caregivers' income. In 2018, caregivers receive 80 per cent of their salary up to a monthly limit of 37,919 SEK (~ 3,792 EUR; ~ 4,346 USD).

present. Some plans, both pedagogical projects with the children and pedagogical reflection meetings for staff, had to be postponed or skipped altogether, so there would be enough staff at least to care for, if not to teach the children.

The municipality's management promoted Lean as a way of structuring and organizing the preschool activities to save time, thereby making more time for the children. And although Unit Head Christina said that it might have seemed unusual to bring a management model from the automotive industry into childcare, the preschool was in desperate need of more time to spend with the children. In that sense, it was an understandable solution. If there were no room in the budget for more teachers, perhaps the solution could be found in increased staff efficiency – one of the goals for bringing Lean into the municipality. The other goals were to provide quality services and create more 'joy at work'. The underlying assumption was that if the employees became more efficient, there would be more time for the users – the children – and therefore the quality of service would automatically increase, resulting in greater joy in the workplace. Many of the preschool teachers in the preschool were optimistic because they hoped that Lean would save more time for them, allowing them to be the pedagogues they wanted to be.

## Meeting ethnography in and the everyday activities of preschools

During fieldwork as a staff member in preschools and conducting fieldwork in numerous meetings at which municipal staff and preschool teachers discussed Lean and used Lean tools, I was drawn into the world of childcare policy, management models, and the world of preschool teachers and children. I became fascinated by the type of knowledge that governed preschools and how the staff tried to fit Lean into the work processes of caring for and educating children. Ben-Ari (2002) has noted that there have been few attempts at studying preschools ethnographically from an organizational perspective with the aim of understanding the relationship between childcare and the specific types of policies that govern preschools. Exceptions are Ben-Ari's (1996, 2002) own work on Japanese childcare, Handelman's (2004) work on the bureaucratic states' visibility in Israeli kindergarten, and the Tobin et al. (2009) comparative study of preschools in China, Japan, and the USA. There is, of course, a whole field of childhood studies (e.g. Shweder 2009) and studies on the anthropology of children and childhood (e.g. Mead 1930 [2009]; Montgomery 2008) that focus on children and children's lives. In relation to preschools, this literature focuses on pedagogy and children's learning rather than the mundane bureaucratic and organizational procedures that form them. I want to draw attention to the organizational aspect of preschools, as I develop an ethnographic account of a Swedish public preschool, the preschool teachers' efforts to make sense of and use the Lean management model to improve their work organization, and the frictions created.

As I mentioned at the beginning of this chapter, the first time I came into contact with Lean in relation to preschools was not as a researcher, but as a parent involved with other parents in a Preschool Council meeting at my son's preschool. My son's preschool had established a Preschool Council to involve parents in its work, and we met once every autumn and spring to do just that. The parents were elected by the parental group, two from each of the four divisions of the preschool. I had been one of those elected, and had been involved for several years. I found it fascinating, not only as a parent, but also as a scholar of organization, bureaucracy, and policy, trying to understand the way preschools were organized and what bureaucratic procedures and policies guided them. It was at one of these meetings that I first heard of Lean. When I finally understood what Unit Head Greta was talking about, I realized that I needed to study the introduction of Lean in preschools as a researcher: How could Lean possibly be applied to preschools?

I began by contacting the administration of a municipality that had introduced Lean management as a tool for making work more efficient, qualitative, and thereby more joyous in its public services, including social services, homecare, care of the elderly and disabled, preschools, and administration. At the same time, I contacted a preschool that was working to introduce Lean. I ended up doing participant observation in two preschool units. The first preschool unit I contacted was Birch Preschool Unit,[7] which included four preschools: Bumblebee, Spider, Grasshopper, and Cricket. In my work with the Lean management model I did participant observation among employees from all four preschools, but it was at Bumblebee Preschool where I spent time among the children working as a staff member, doing participant observation. I also did fieldwork in Elm Preschool Unit, which included six preschools, in one of which, Ladybug Preschool, I did participant observation as a staff member working with the children. But I did participant observation among employees in two other Elm Preschool Unit preschools: Butterfly and Caterpillar.

Once I had established rapport through interviews, it was relatively easy to gain access to Lean management activities in the municipality in general and preschools in particular. I started out in February 2012 to begin my participant observation in two management group meetings at the Birch Preschool Unit, just as the preschool heads of the four preschools in the unit were trying to make sense of some of the tools of the Lean management model. I also interviewed the development strategist at the municipality, whose job it was to ensure that Lean was implemented within the entire municipality, including social services, homecare, care of the elderly and disabled, preschools, and

---

7 All names are anonymized: preschool units, preschools, preschool teachers, and the few children I mention. I have chosen tree names for the preschool units and insect names for the preschools within the preschool units, as it is not unusual for Swedish preschool units to be named after something in the environment.

administration. I attended a three-day course on how to become a Lean coach in the municipality. The Lean coaches were municipal administrators, social workers, homecare workers, caregivers to the elderly and disabled, and preschool teachers. These employees, who had expressed interest in being part of the municipality's investment in converting to a Lean organization, worked part-time as Lean coaches in the municipality. I did fieldwork in several meetings and attended the Lean Forum meeting, where all the Lean coaches in the municipality met to discuss their work and were updated on Lean and its methods. I accompanied the development strategist to a Lean Network meeting, which included participants responsible for Lean in other municipalities, attended other Lean meetings, and interviewed Unit Head Christina in the preschool where I had taken part in the management group meetings.

I have referred to fieldwork in meetings as 'punctuate entries' (Thedvall 2013) because of their unique, punctuated character in a challenging data collection context. I sat in the meetings as a participant, but primarily observed and took notes. The fieldwork in the meetings gave me a deeper understanding of how Lean was used within the municipality and particularly in preschools. I wondered how Lean was played out in the day-to-day activities of the preschool, however. Did they actually use Lean, and how did it affect the organization of work in the preschool? Having become familiar with my work, Unit Head Christina and Preschool Heads Sigrid, Angelica, Nina, and Michael of Birch Preschool Unit agreed to my doing participant observation as a member of the staff in Bumblebee Preschool as long as the parents agreed. I made it clear in a letter that the object of study was the organization of preschool activities rather than the children, and none of the parents objected.

I was unable to do long-term participant observation, but I did manage to stay in Bumblebee Preschool for two weeks in September 2013 and another two weeks in October 2013. When I was participating in the Lean Forum in the municipality, I met one of the Lean coaches from the Elm Preschool Unit, and she suggested I come to them, so I spent two weeks in November 2013 in Ladybug Preschool. The fact that my child was in preschool between 2008 and 2013 was valuable to my understanding of the organization and the terminology of Swedish public preschools. Together with my previous fieldwork in Lean meetings, it proved crucial in gaining a fuller understanding of the organization, the jargon, the discussions, the implications of these discussions in the everyday activities of preschools.

My interest in preschool activities resonated with my interest in bureaucracy and organization. My focus on the organization of preschool activities was also based on the fact that the municipality understood the use of Lean as a way to make the organization of work more 'effective' and 'qualitative', thereby creating more 'joy at work'. It was the organization of work that was the target. This meant that I wanted to participate in the day-to-day activities, taking care of and teaching the children, but I also wanted to participate in the planning and organization of these activities. I ended up spending about one-third of my fieldwork in meetings – about 5 hours a week. This did not correspond to the time the preschool teachers spent in meetings. The preschools were separated into divisions,[8] and I attended the weekly planning meetings of all four divisions and the weekly meetings of the division heads at Bumblebee Preschool. These meetings gave me a good overview of how the work was organized in the entire preschool system. Bumblebee Preschool also had monthly two-hour workplace meetings, three of which I attended – two as a staff member and one after I had finished my fieldwork as a staff member, but had joined in for follow-up meetings on a Lean action plan. On Mondays and Fridays the teachers had other planning meetings: the two-hour pedagogical development group meeting on Mondays and the two-hour pedagogical reflection meeting on Fridays where I learnt more about the everyday activities of preschools. And then Lean introduced another set of meetings, focusing on its tools and its strategies for improvement.

I spent most of my time in the 2- to 3-year-old and the 5- to 6-year-old divisions in Bumblebee Preschool and with the 3- to 4-year-olds in Ladybug Preschool, because these were the understaffed divisions at the time of my fieldwork. I did the work of any other *unqualified* teacher – which is the term for teachers without education as either a teacher assistant[9] or a preschool teacher. Public preschools preferably had a mix of preschool teachers and teacher assistants, but most of them also employed 'unqualified' or non-certified teachers as I will refer to them because there were not enough educated teachers.[10] Preschool teachers had a minimum of a Bachelor's degree in early childhood education; teacher assistants had a senior-high-school diploma in childcare, and non-certified staff members have neither accreditation, although they may be high school or university graduates in another field. When I use the term

---

8 Swedish public preschools are often divided into 'divisions'. In some preschools, the children are placed in a particular division because of their age, which was the case in the preschools where I conducted my fieldwork. In some preschools, they are placed in what is referred to as sibling groups, with other children who may be between one and six years old. I describe this system in greater detail in Chapter 4.

9 The Swedish term *barnskötare* can also be translated into childcare assistant or child minder, but these terms are misleading, because *barnskötare* often do the same pedagogical work as university-educated preschool teachers, even if they do not have the same responsibilities for pedagogical work as the preschool teachers have. I have chosen the term 'teacher assistant', because it reflects the pedagogical work they do better than the term 'childcare assistant' does.

10 Statistics from 2014 (there are no statistics available from 2013 when I did fieldwork) conclude that 31 per cent of the preschool employees in the municipality where I did fieldwork were university educated (compared to 24 per cent in privately owned preschools in the same area), 33 per cent had a high school diploma in childcare (compared to 31 per cent in private preschools), and 36 per cent were non-certified teachers (compared to 45 per cent in private preschools). www.jmftal.artisan.se/databas.aspx?presel#tab-0 (accessed June 2018). Data collected from the Swedish National Agency for Education.

'preschool teachers' or 'teacher',[11] it includes all three categories of staff members because, in practice, there is little difference in the caregiving and pedagogical work that the incumbents of these three categories do, although the preschool teachers are responsible for ensuring that the preschool is following the Preschool Curriculum.

As a non-certified preschool teacher, I cared for the children, and along with the other teachers, made sure their diapers were changed or they had gone to the toilet, ensured that they had food, had their afternoon nap, helped them take off their outer garments when they came in from the preschool yard and put them on when they were going outside. I played with the children in the preschool yard, and inside the building. I talked to the children, stopped fights and arguments (more or less successfully), laughed with them – and one time, not my finest moment, I scolded them in a way I'm not very proud of. I tried to imitate the way the teachers spoke to the children in the preschool, by not saying 'Don't run in the corridor', but saying what they should do: 'In the corridor, we walk'. Easier said than done, but still . . . I also participated in the teaching, assisting the teachers doing pedagogical projects with the children, and attempted to mimic the way the preschool teachers wove pedagogy into the everyday activities of preschools – also more or less successfully. The teachers taught me how to work with problematic children using the five-coin method, or five of anything, which required reprimanded children being shown that I loved them times five (Forster 2009). Working with people who make it their job to care for and teach our young children has taught me the utmost respect for and importance of this profession.

Participant observation as a staff member gave me a deeper understanding of the work practices, the jargon, and the organization of the preschool, but it was in the Lean meetings and other types of meetings, such as the weekly meetings, and the monthly workplace meetings that the organization of work in the preschool was discussed and negotiated. Because I was interested in discussions and negotiations around the planning and the organization process of preschool activities, these meetings were where I needed to be. Meetings were also part of the everyday activities of preschools, part of being a teacher, as much as caring for and teaching children. And it was in the Lean meetings that the discussions on how to become a Lean, effective organization were formulated with the help of the Lean tools. And it was in the Lean meetings that I came to understand the direction in which the Lean management model moved discussions and affected practices – in directions often not executed, but planned.

For this reason, the ethnographic descriptions in this book are often played out in meetings, in what Jen Sandler and I have called 'meeting ethnography' (Sandler and Thedvall 2017). To an ethnographer interested in the organization

---

11 The Swedish term *pedagoger* (pedagogues) includes all three categories and was the term they used when referring to themselves.

of work in preschools and the introduction of the Lean management model – the discussion, negotiations, plans, and decisions – the meetings turned out to be a valuable place for investigation.

## Outline of the book

The tensions between the dispositions of the Lean model, the dispositions of preschool work, and the requirements of the preschool work are explored throughout each chapter. Each chapter focuses on a particular theoretically grounded empirical issue from my study. Chapters 2 and 3 set the scene, with an examination and analysis of the policy words and meetings of preschools and management models. Chapters 4–6 each focus on three areas essential to the Lean management model – colours, flow, and plans. I use these tools to bring the concepts to life in relation to the care and education of children and the ongoing way of organizing everyday work processes in Swedish preschools. These chapters introduce the Lean management model and the new environments of power it creates. They also question the underlying idea behind the management model: that organizational structure can be separated and abstracted from organizational work.

Chapter 2, *Words: The Policy Words of Preschools and Management Models*, addresses words, particularly the policy words used to guide and steer organizational practices. Policy words are meant to do things in the world (Gluck and Tsing 2009); they are formulated and fashioned to steer and govern. I understand policy words as objects. Compared to other words, policy words have a thing-ified quality in the writing of policies and organizational guidance (Urla 2012). Policy words often come in semantic clusters (Shore and Wright 1997), making management models such as Lean an empirical fact. This chapter explores how Lean policy words fit into the everyday organization of preschools and what they signal and mobilize. Ethnographically, the chapter is placed in the 'unplanned' activities and the management group meetings in the preschool. The 'unplanned' activities illustrate how preschool teachers interpret the everyday activities of learning and caring in relation to the Preschool Curriculum and Reggio Emilia. Lean management meetings illustrate the policy words that comprise the Lean management model in relation to the organization of preschools. The chapter also shows the 'language work' (Tamm Hallström and Thedvall 2015) involved, not only when attempting to implement Lean words and its values in preschools, but also in the organization of preschool in general.

Chapter 3, *Meetings: Lean Meetings and Preschool Circle Time*, focuses on the meeting as a practice of performing policy words and language work, imbuing specific policy values into children and preschool teachers. The meeting is a place for practicing policy, but the meeting itself also practices policy through its organization, the instruments used, and the material artefact it includes. In this way, the meeting makes not only policy, but also policy subjects and policy environments. It is through the meeting that the Lean model, as an example of Latour's 'immutable mobile' is abstracted and transported. This includes the specific ideas, language, technologies, and actors involved. It is through the meeting that Lean becomes an event-that-models. Ethnographically the chapter focuses on a Lean improvement-group meeting, a pedagogical reflection meeting, and the children's circle-time meeting, in which songs are sung and attendance is taken. Sandler and I (Sandler and Thedvall 2017) have developed an analytical framework for analysing meetings, wherein we understand meetings as involving 'architecture', 'practices of circulation', and 'makers'. The focus of this chapter is on meetings and on architectural and material construct, through its templates and procedures and through its practices of circulation through the ideas, language, activities, power, and decision-making that circulate in the meeting. It also focuses on the meeting as a 'maker' of governance and management.

Chapter 4, *Colour: Colours at Work in Play and in Management*, explores the evaluation of 'joy at work' among the preschool staff members through the Lean colours of green, yellow, and red. In the automotive industry, Lean sets targets for the number of automobiles that should be produced – targets that are made visual on a board, their status tracked by green, yellow, and red symbols, where green signifies that the target has been met, yellow is a warning that the production is starting to fall behind, and red indicates that the automobile production is missing the target. In preschools, the same colours are used to measure joy at work. This chapter compares the use of colours in preschools to their use in the Lean management model, by focusing on the role of colour in organizational practice. By turning attention to the agency of colour, I want to shed light on its operations and power in Swedish public preschools, and in so doing, investigate the agentive powers of colours. This means that I must pay attention to the multiplex political forces that colours both reveal and produce as they compose commanding elements of apparently mundane evaluative bureaucratic practices. Ethnographically, the chapter addresses the role of colours in children's play and pedagogy and their role as a Lean monitoring tool. It is also placed in a Lean staff meeting as the teachers evaluate their workweek through colours.

Chapter 5, *Flow: eliminating waste along the assembly line*, investigates flows in preschools and management models. It focuses on Lean's premise of efficient flows, the elimination of waste in the Lean management model, and how flow and waste are played out in preschools. The notion of efficient flows highlights what Rosa (2017) calls 'the escalatory logic of modernity', in that modernity requires systematic growth, innovation, and acceleration, making room for 'fast policy' (Peck and Theodore 2015a). The promise that smooth flows and efficiency would eliminate waste gives Lean 'model power' (Peck and Theodore 2015b). I argue that Lean is a socially produced smoothing machine (Bogard 2000), set to smooth flows by eradicating waste in production processes. The main focus is the dynamic and performative role played by waste in making efficient flows in the Lean smoothing machine and how it relates to preschools. Ethnographically, the chapter explains how the movement of children is organized, as they move from the yard into the preschool. The chapter takes the reader to a Lean coach-training course, through where I learnt about the importance of flow and efficiency from Lean's point of view and it is set in a Lean meeting where preschool staff members are set to make the preschool yard flow smoothly.

Chapter 6, *Plan: Hoping for an Efficient Future*, examines plans and planning in preschools. It focuses on the hope produced by the Lean action plan of turning current states into desired states. The notion of a plan has a temporal aspect, promising something for the future. In this way, it is intimately connected to hope. Plans can control, oppress, change, or improve, but inherent in plans are hopes for a better future, even if it is in the name of oppression. I pay attention to what plans do as they make promises about the future (Abram and Weszkalnys 2013: 9). The main focus is on the affective and performative role played by plans in the Lean model, and to the way it relates to preschools. I treat hopes and plans as ethnographic categories for critical analysis (cf. Kleist and Jansen 2016). I am interested in the agentive powers of hope in creating imagined futures when Lean plans are made. It is the performative role of plans and their ability to provoke affective responses that is investigated here in relation to Lean and the organization of preschools. The main focus is what plans and hope *do* in preschools. Ethnographically, the chapter explores preschool planning and action in relation to Lean action plans and preschool teachers' attempts to turn Lean plans into action.

Chapter 7, *Conclusion: the utopia of efficiency*. In the final chapter, I return to the theoretical questions that framed this study and discuss model friction, model utopia, model acceleration, model power, and model failure in relation to policy words, meetings, colours, flows, and plans. I analyse the tensions between the easy to use and difficult to use in management models. I discuss the relationships among the chapters and the social effects of Lean in the preschool context. Particular focus is placed on the pedagogical assignment that has been set for the preschools and the need to separate the pedagogical and the organizational in the Lean model in order to make the model work. This situation is discussed in relation to the idea that Lean creates more time with the children. Moving beyond these questions, I explore the utopian dimension of the modern project in pursuit of efficiency and speed in relation to the Lean model and the preschool teachers' work, asking 'What are the wider societal implications of the Lean project?'

# References

Abram, Simone and Weszkalnys, Gisa (2013), *Elusive promises: Planning in the contemporary world* (Oxford, UK: Berghahn Books).

Appadurai, Arjun (1996), *Modernity at large: Cultural dimensions of globalization* (Public worlds, 99-3013247-3; 1; Minneapolis: University of Minnesota Press).

Bear, Laura and Mathur, Nayanika (2015), 'Introduction: Remaking the public good: A new anthropology of bureaucracy', *The Cambridge Journal of Anthropology*, 33 (1), 18–34.

Ben-Ari, Eyal (1996), *Japanese childcare: An interpretive study of culture and organization* (Japanese studies (London), 99-0575705-8; London: Kegan Paul).

——— (2002), 'State standardisation and "normal" children: An anthropological study of a preschool', in Roger Goodman (ed.), *Family and social policy in Japan: Anthropological approaches* (Cambridge: Cambridge University Press), 111–130.

Bogard, William (2000), 'Smoothing machines and the constitution of society', *Cultural Studies*, 14 (2), 269–294.

Brunsson, Nils and Sahlin-Andersson, Kerstin (2000), 'Constructing organizations: The case of public sector reform', *Organization Studies*, 21 (4), 721–746.

Czarniawska, Barbara and Sevón, Guje (eds.) (1996), *Translating organizational change* (de Gruyter studies in organization, 99-0475868-9; 56; Berlin: de Gruyter).

Drucker, Peter (1954 [2007]), *The Practice of management* (Oxford: Black and White).

Edwards, Carolyn P., Gandini, Lella, and Forman, George E. (eds.) (2012), *The hundred languages of children: The Reggio Emilia experience in transformation* (Third edn.; Oxford: Praeger).

Ferguson, James (1990), *The anti-politics machine: "Development," depoliticization and bureaucratic power in Lesotho* (Minneapolis: University of Minnesota Press).

Forster, Martin (2009), *Fem gånger mer kärlek. Forskning och praktiska råd för ett fungerande familjeliv – en bok till föräldrar med barn mellan 2 och 12 år* (Stockholm: Natur & kultur).

Gal, Susan (2015), 'Politics of translation', *Annual Review of Anthropology*, 44 (1), 225–240.

Garsten, Christina, Lindvert, Jessica, Jambrén, Niklas, and Thedvall, Renita. (2006), 'From employment to the development of workers' capabilities: Mobility, learning and responsibility in Swedish worklife', (Report for the European Commission).

Garsten, Christina, Lindvert, Jessica, and Thedvall, Renita (eds.) (2015), *Makeshift work in a changing labour market: The Swedish model in the post-financial crisis era* (Cheltenham: Edward Elgar).

Geertz, Clifford (1973), *The interpretation of cultures: Selected essays* (New York: Basic Books).

Gluck, Carol and Tsing, Anna Lowenhaupt (2009), *Words in motion: Toward a global lexicon* (Durham: Duke University Press).

Hall, Patrik (2008), *Managementbyråkrati: Organisationspolitisk makt i svensk offentlig förvaltning* (Malmö: Liber).

Handelman, Don (2004), *Nationalism and the Israeli state: Bureaucratic logic in public events* (Oxford: Berg).

Hannerz, Ulf (1992), *Cultural complexity: Studies in the social organization of meaning* (New York: Columbia University Press).

——— (1996), *Transnational connections: Culture, people, places* (London: Routledge).

Hood, Christopher (1991), 'A public management for all seasons?', *Public Administration*, 69 (1), 3–19.

Huczynski, Andrzej (1993), *Management gurus. What makes them and how to become one* (London: Routledge).

James, Allison (2012), 'Child-centredness' and "the child": The cultural politics of Nursery Schooling in England', in Anne Trine Kjørholt and Jens Qvortrup (eds.), *The modern child and the flexible labour market: Early childhood education and care* (New York: Palgrave Macmillan), 111–127.

Kleist, Nauja and Jansen, Stef (2016), 'Introduction: Hope over time: Crisis, immobility and future-making', *History and Anthropology*, 27 (4), 373–392.

Latour, Bruno (1986), 'Visualisation and cognition: Drawing things together', in Henrika Kuklick and Elizabeth Long (eds.), *Knowledge and society: Studies in the sociology of culture past and present* (6; Greenwich, CT: JAI Press).
——— (1987), *Science in action: How to follow scientists and engineers through society* (Harvard: Harvard university press).
——— (1996), *Aramis or the love of technology* (Cambridge, MA: Harvard University Press).
Li, Tania Murray (2007), *The will to improve: Governmentality, development, and the practice of politics* (Durham: Duke University Press).
Liker, Jeffrey K. (2004), *The Toyota way: 14 management principles from the world's greatest manufacturer* (London: McGraw-Hill).
Mead, Margaret (1930 [2009]), *Coming of age in Samoa: A psychological study of primitive youth for western civilisation* (New York: Harper Perennial).
Modig, Niklas and Åhlström, Pär (2012), *This is lean: Resolving the efficiency paradox* (Stockholm: Rheologica Publishing).
Montgomery, Heather (2008), *An introduction to childhood: Anthropological perspectives on children's lives* (Hoboken, NJ: John Wiley & Sons).
Moss, Peter (2012), 'Governed markets and democratic experimentalism: Two possibilities for early childhood education and care', in Anne Trine Kjørholt and Jens Qvortrup (eds.), *The modern child and the flexible labour market: Early childhood education and care* (New York: Palgrave Macmillan), 128–149.
Neuman, Michelle J. (2009), 'The politics of (de) centralisation: Early care and education in France and Sweden', in Kirsten Scheiwe and Harry Willekens (eds.), *Childcare and preschool development in Europe: Institutional perspective* (New York: Palgrave Macmillan), 157–179.
Peck, Jamie and Theodore, Nik (2015a), *Fast policy: Experimental statecraft at the thresholds of neoliberalism* (Minneapolis: University of Minnesota Press).
——— (2015b), 'Paying for good behavior: Cash transfer policies in the wild', in Ananya Roy and Emma Shaw Crane (eds.), *Territories of poverty: Rethinking north and south* (Athens: University of Georgia Press).
Peters, Thomas J. and Waterman, Robert H. (1982), *In search of excellence. Lessons from America's best-run companies* (New York: Harper and Row).
Power, Michael (1997), *The audit society: Rituals of verification* (Oxford: Oxford University Press).
Preschool Curriculum (2011), 'Curriculum for the Preschool Lpfö 98 revised 2010', in Skolverket (Swedish National Agency for Education) (ed.) (Stockholm).
Rosa, Hartmut (2013), *Social acceleration: A new theory of modernity* (New York: Columbia University Press).
——— (2017), 'De-synchronization, dynamic stabilization, dispositional squeeze', in Judy Wajcman and Nigel Dodd (eds.), *The sociology of speed: Digital, organizational, and social temporalities* (Oxford: Oxford University Press), 25–41.
Rose, Nicolas and Miller, Peter (1992), 'Political power beyond the state: Problematics of government', *British Journal of Sociology*, 43 (2), 172–205.
Røvik, Kjell Arne (2000), *Moderna organisationer: Trender inom organisationstänkandet vid millennieskiftet* (Malmö: Liber).
Sahlin-Andersson, Kerstin (1996), 'Imitating by editing success: The construction of organizational fields and identities', in Barbara Czarniawska and Guje Sevón (eds.), *Translating organizational change* (Berlin: Walter de Gruyter).
——— (2001), 'National, international and transnational constructions of new public management', in Tom Christensen and Per Laegreid (eds.), *New public management: The transformation of ideas and practice* (Aldershot: Ashgate).

Sahlin-Andersson, Kerstin and Engwall, Lars (eds.) (2002), *The expansion of management knowledge: Carriers, flows, and sources* (Stanford: Stanford University Press).

Sandler, Jen and Thedvall, Renita (eds.) (2017), *Meeting ethnography: Meetings as key technologies of contemporary governance, development, and resistance* (Routledge studies in anthropology series; New York: Routledge).

Scott, James C. (1998), *Seeing like a state: How certain schemes to improve the human condition have failed* (Yale agrarian studies; New Haven: Yale University Press).

Senge, Peter (1994 [2006]), *The Fifth Discipline: The art and practice of the learning organization* (London: Random House Books).

SFS, Swedish Statutes (1973:1205), 'Preschool act', Swedish Parliament (Sveriges Riksdag).

——— (1980:620), 'Social services act', Swedish Parliament (Sveriges Riksdag).

——— (1997:1212), 'Education act', Swedish Parliament (Sveriges Riksdag).

——— (2010:800), 'Education act', in Swedish Parliament (Sveriges Riksdag).

Shore, Cris and Wright, Susan (1997), *Anthropology of policy: Perspectives on governance and power* (London: Routledge).

——— (2000), 'Coercive accountability: The rise of audit culture in higher education', in Marilyn Strathern (ed.), *Audit cultures: Anthropological studies in accountability, ethics and the academy* (London: Routledge), 69–101.

——— (2011), 'Conceptualising policy: Technologies of governance and the politics of visibility', in Cris Shore, Susan Wright and Davide Però (eds.), *Policy worlds: Anthropology and the analysis of contemporary power* (Oxford: Berghahn Books), 1–25.

——— (2015), 'Audit culture revisited: Rankings, ratings, and the reassembling of society', *Current Anthropology*, 56 (3), 431–432.

Shweder, Richard A. (ed.) (2009), *The child: An encyclopedic companion* (Chicago: University of Chicago Press).

Strang, David and Meyer, John W. (1993), 'Institutional conditions for diffusion', *Theory and Society*, 22 (4), 487–511.

Strathern, Marilyn (2000), *Audit cultures: Anthropological studies in accountability, ethics, and the academy* (London: Routledge).

Tamm Hallström, Kristina and Thedvall, Renita (2015), 'Managing administrative reform through language work: Implementing Lean in Swedish public sector organisations', *Scandinavian Journal of Public Administration*, 19 (2), 89–108.

Thedvall, Renita (2013), 'Punctuated entries: Doing fieldwork in policy meetings in the European Union', in Christina Garsten and Anette Nyqvist (eds.), *Organisational anthropology: Doing ethnography in and among complex organisations* (London: Pluto Press), 106–119.

Tobin, Joseph, Hsueh, Yeh, and Karasawa, Mayumi (2009), *Preschool in three cultures revisited: China, Japan, and the United States* (Chicago: University of Chicago Press).

Urban, Greg (2001), *Metaculture: How culture moves through the world* (Minneapolis: University of Minnesota Press).

Urla, Jacqueline (2012), 'Total quality language revival', in Monica Heller and Duchêne (eds.), *Language in late capitalism: Pride and profit* (New York: Routledge), 73–92.

Womack, James P. and Jones, Daniel T. (1996), *Lean thinking: Banish waster and create wealth in your corporation* (New York: Simon & Schuster).

Womack, James P., Jones, Daniel T., and Roos, Daniel (1990), *Machine that changed the world: How Lean production revolutionized the global car wars* (New York: Simon & Schuster).

Wurm, Julianne (2005), *Working in the Reggio way: A beginner's guide for American teachers* (St. Paul, Minnesota: Redleaf Press).

Chapter 2

# Words

## The policy words of preschools and management models

This chapter is about words: the policy words used to guide and steer organizational practices – words that are meant to do things in the world (Gluck and Tsing 2009). Policy words, formulated and fashioned to steer and govern, often come in clusters. Shore and Wright (1997) have written about semantic clusters of such policy words as effective, quality, benchmarking, empowerment, and continuous improvements, forming policy ideals of what to do, how to think, and how to guide and steer organizational practices. Policy words, in this sense, work as 'keywords' in Raymond Williams's (1976) meaning of the term: 'they are significant, binding words in certain activities and their interpretation; they are significant, indicative words in certain forms of thought' (p. 13). Shore and Wright (1997) discuss the role and power of semantic clusters that become vehicles for mobilizing and signalling new patterns of governance, but also for influencing the minds and subjectivities of employees (Foucault 1988, 1991; Martin 1997; Oakes et al. 1998). As semantic clusters, policy words work like instruments, introducing regimes of thought into environments – in this case into preschools. What values and patterns of governance are introduced when Lean policy words enter preschool pedagogy and curriculum principles? What are the existing semantic clusters of policy words, and what regimes of thought do they project? How do these words and regimes relate to the clusters of Lean policy words? How is this 'language work'[1] (Tamm Hallström and Thedvall 2015) performed when attempting to implement Lean words and its value in preschools?

I argue in this chapter that Lean policy words make the Lean management model an empirical fact, shaping the conditions of the organization – in this case, preschools. I draw on Latour's (1986) work on immutable mobiles and on the work of Holmes (2014), who argues, in relation to central bankers, that the words, the statements, the communication of central bank policies is part

---

1 I am not referring to the type of language work discussed by Heller (2010), Shankar and Cavanaugh (2012), and Urciuoli and LaDousa (2013), which is about language qualified as *the* work, and in this sense made into a commodity, a skill, a capital, such as in call centres. It has also been called language labour (Urciuoli and LaDousa 2013). I refer to the deliberate and intentional process, work, with language, with words, in the Lean management model to create a Lean regime of thought.

22  Words

*Table 2.1* Policy words of Lean and preschools – some will be put into context and explained in this chapter; others will be explained in the chapters to follow

| Lean policy words | Swedish preschool policy words |
| --- | --- |
| Eliminating waste | Reggio-Emilia pedagogy |
| Flow efficiency | Gender equality |
| Continuous improvement | Democracy |
| Just-in-time production | Group learning |
| Evaluation | Co-operation |
| Monitoring | Lifelong learning |
| *Autonomation* | Human rights |
| Customer pull | Solidarity |
| *Andon* | Tolerance |
| Lean board meetings | Non-discrimination |
| Improvement board | Respect for differences |
| Performance management board | The hundred languages |
| Improvement-group meeting | Information board |
| Value-stream mapping | Arranging the day |
| Flow unit | Pedagogical documentation |
| Cycle time | Pedagogist |
| Value-added time/non-value-added time | Pedagogical reflection meetings |
| A3 | Planning time |
| Action plan | Planning meetings |
| 5S | Circle time |
| 8 wastes | Pedagogical project |
| Lean coach | Third teacher |
| PDCA | Pedagogical year |
| 5 Whys | Pedagogical cafe |
| Current state/desired state | Pee and poo chart |
| Project plan | Play area |
| Implementation plan | APT |

of making the economy an empirical fact. In the same way, the communication of management model policy words makes the model present and possible in the preschool. These words – these 'instruments of persuasion' as Holmes (2014) calls them – are not mere representations of the economy. Rather, they *create* the economy – what Holmes (2009) calls the 'economy of words'. He claims that these market regimes – or, in his case, monetary regimes – are created through the architects (through the process of writing technical reports, policy statements, and presentations) in collaboration with the public. It is in collaboration with the economy of words and the public's actions taken in relation to these words that together shape the economic and monetary conditions (Holmes 2014). The Central Bank needs to maintain public confidence in the currency in order to create monetary stability, and that task is performed through words (Holmes 2014). In a similar fashion, through presentations of Lean, the Lean coaches in the municipality need to use Lean words and to distribute books about the wonders of Lean in order to maintain the preschool teachers' confidence in the Lean management model – that it can solve all their organizational problems and save time. It is in this collaborative mode that the Lean regime of thought is created and recreated.

In the first part of this chapter, I present my view on what words are and what they can do. I propose that policy words have a 'thing-ified' quality (Urla 2012) that makes them moveable across organizational worlds. In the following section, I present the policy words of the Lean model and how it is set to work in the automotive industry. I then turn to the policy words active in the setting of Swedish preschools, with comparisons to the USA and the UK, with particular focus on the public preschools where I conducted my fieldwork. I then turn to the ways in which policy words guide and organize preschool activities in Sweden, by describing everyday life in preschools. In the final section, I present how Lean clusters of policy words have moved into different industries and services around the world, ending up in Swedish public preschools. In the conclusion, I discuss the policy words of management models and preschool policy documents, comparing values and goals, pointing to the power inherent in the mobility of management models.

## Moveable words with a thing-ified quality

Words are material (e.g. Shankar and Cavanaugh 2012). This is especially true for policy words, in that they are the 'objectualization of language' (Silverstein 1996), with an alienable quality making them moveable as material objects, changing ownership, sometimes possible to circulate as commodities (Duchêne and Heller 2012; Heller 2010; Shankar and Cavanaugh 2012) or as words that aim to set political standards in the world (Gluck and Tsing 2009). It is this material character that makes clusters of policy words into immutable mobile (Latour 1986) models, possible to move around the world and able to exercise power over many places that are distant in space and time. As İslamoğlu (2009: 265) writes:

> The very nature of words in motions is that words suddenly find themselves embedded in power relations different from those with which they were initially associated. In this sense, words are not merely signifiers but also agents that help create new environments of power and as such implicated in the contradictions that attend such processes of transformation.

The transformation in question may not be the action intended by policymakers. Policy words can make divergent actions possible. In this sense, policy words are multi-vocal. They show the direction, but they are open for interpretation. In Gallie's (1955) terms, policy words are 'essentially contested concepts'. One of the powers of policy words lies in the fact that they are able to harbour different interpretations. Still, the choice of policy words, independently and collectively, reveals the values and ideals embedded in the policy that produces specific regimes of thought. They guide the direction towards what are perceived to be relevant problems and appropriate solutions to certain forms of complications. As Shankar and Cavanaugh (2012) write: 'As objectifications circulate and are taken up in new contexts, they may transform social meanings, relationships, and values, as well as form connections between everyday contexts of talk and other types of circulations' (p. 361). In this sense, policy words are performative.

Holmes (2014) introduces a collaborative aspect into his version of performativity, which I find useful. He is drawing on Callon's (1995, 1998) understanding of the economy as being continuously formed, shaped, and performed, rather than something 'out there' and observable. As Callon (1995, 1998) famously explained, economists perform and shape the economy through economic theory. Callon (1995, 1998) studied the performativity of economic theories in relation to markets, but Holmes focused on the policies and the words that shape them and their performative work in relation to public action forming the economy. Performativity in this sense of the term springs out of the tradition of John Langshaw Austin's (1962) language philosophy and the idea that utterances are performative – that words are a performance of action. I understand words to be performance of action, and, in the same vein, words as practice. It is through the performative collaborative mode of Lean policy words by the preschool teachers' interaction with them that the Lean regime of thought is created.

## Lean policy words in the automotive factory

The policy words of the Lean management model have grown out of the process of developing the 'Toyota Production System' in the Toyota car manufacturing plant in Japan (Ohno 1988). James P. Womack, Daniel T. Jones, and Daniel Roos introduced the model to their English-speaking audience in their 1990 bestseller, *The Machine That Changed the World*. Womack et al. (1990) had performed research on the Toyota model of organizing automotive production and the mass-production model à la Ford, and through their research demonstrated that the Toyota model was much more successful than the Ford–Sloan, mass-production techniques. Womack et al. wanted to spread their insights via their book and adopted the term 'Lean production' to signal the change from mass production. As Womack et al. (1990: 11) wrote:

> Lean production (a term coined by IMVP researcher John Krafcik) is 'lean' because it uses less of everything compared with mass production – half

the human effort in the factory, half the engineering hours to develop a new product in half the time. Also, it requires keeping far less than half the needed inventory on site.

Womack et al. (1990) presented the story of Lean production and explained how Eiji Toyoda and Taiichi Ohno started the work on the 'Toyota Production System' (TPS) in the 1950s. In 1978, Taiichi Ohno (1988) published *Toyota Production System*, which was later published in English. The original idea of the Toyota production system was based on the elimination of waste, and rested on two pillars. (1) The *just-in-time production* introduced a smooth-flowing production process wherein every part in the production reaches the production line 'just in time' to keep cost of inventory down and eliminate production line delays. (2) Ohno called the other pillar *autonomation*: automation with a human touch or giving human intelligence to the machine. In the Toyota plant, autonomation meant that humans should supervise the machines so they could detect malfunctions early and push the stop button to minimize waste. This scheme was then expanded to the manually operated parts of the production line, so that workers could push the button when detecting abnormalities (Ohno 1988). The idea of stopping the entire production line was also to establish that everyone was aware of the problem, and could eliminate waste by preventing overproduction and the production of defective products.

In the development of Lean production, Womack and Jones (1996) established that Lean was governed by five principles: (1) Specify value from the customers' perspective; (2) map the value stream to understand value and non-value added steps; (3) flow the work through the processes in the value stream; (4) schedule the work based on customer pull;[2] and (5) strive for perfection through continuous improvement and eliminating waste. Liker (2004) later introduced the idea that Lean comprises 14 principles that guide the model and its tools. These 14 principles were built on Ohno's and on Womack and Jones's work in pushing for smooth-flowing value streams, continuous improvement, and elimination of waste, which together form the basis for the model. These were the 14 principles being taught in Lean's coach-training course that I participated in when I was doing research within the municipality. It was being discussed as a philosophy – the Lean philosophy that should be ingrained in employees. Consultants pushing the idea that Lean is 80 per cent philosophy and 20 per cent tools taught the 14 principles that appeared in the Lean handbook. It was Lean's policy words in the 14 principles that made the Lean management model an empirical fact set to shape the conditions of

---

[2] According to Lean thinking, companies let the customer pull the product from them as needed, rather than pushing products onto customers.

the organization. In the next part, I present the principles in chunks, followed by further explanation:

1. Base your management decisions on a long-term philosophy, even at the expense of short-term financial goals.
2. Create a continuous process flow to bring problems to the surface.

Principles 1 and 2, which go back to Ohno's autonomation, require that all factory employees are responsible for ensuring that problems are brought to the fore. Principles 3 and 4 have to do with workload and overproduction: that automobiles are produced not only on demand, but also to verify that the workload is levelled out among staff members, so that the assembly line is flowing smoothly.

3. Use 'pull' systems to avoid overproduction.
4. Level out the workload.

Principles 5, 6, 7, and 8 have to do with establishing that there is no waste. These principles introduce the notion that quality should be produced the first time, so that there are no problems from the beginning. And that the goal is reached by standardizing tasks and processes through visual control and the help of all employees, so every problem is brought to the fore, and the right technology is used to serve people and processes.

5. Build a culture of stopping to fix problems, to get quality right the first time.
6. Standardised tasks and processes are the foundation for continuous improvement and employee empowerment.
7. Use visual control so no problems are hidden.
8. Use only reliable, thoroughly tested technology that serves your people and processes.

Principles 9, 10, 11, and 12 have to do with the type of leadership required and how the leaders should think about junior employees, partners, and suppliers. Leaders, junior employees, partners, and suppliers should always be willing to improve (cf. Li 2007) and to work on further improvements.

9. Grow leaders who thoroughly understand the work, live the philosophy, and teach it to others.
10. Develop exceptional people and teams who follow your company's philosophy.
11. Respect your extended network of partners and suppliers by challenging them and helping them improve.
12. Go and see for yourself to thoroughly understand the situation.

The final two principles refer to the ideal Lean organization.

13 Make decisions slowly by consensus, thoroughly considering all options; implement decisions rapidly.
14 Become a learning organisation through relentless reflection and continuous improvement.

(Jeffrey K. Liker 2004: 35ff)

Both the 5-principle model and the 14-principle model emphasized efficient value streams and flows, the focus on customer value and customer pull, and continuous improvements to eliminate waste. The principles formed a semantic cluster of policy words that encouraged organizations to create problem-identifying processes; make slow decisions, but with fast action; and foster an exceptional, active, learning employee who gets it right the first time and makes continuous improvements through the standardization of tasks and visualization techniques to improve flow efficiency. The assembly line was understood as a flow, in which the car should go through, moving between various stations as efficiently as possible, eliminating any elements in the work process that do not add value.

The Lean management model has more in common with scientific management (Taylor 1911) than with the post-Fordist era of 'flexible specialization' (Harvey 1990). Lean focuses on efficient flows rather than flexibility, but with the ideals of the 'enterprising self' (Rose 1992). The model brings a peculiar mix of policy words that establish a new management ideal of the modern, efficient assembly line, to which every employee mechanically adds a small piece to the production process, and the postmodern flexible employee who strives to fulfil the efficient flow and is expected to adapt to the model and continuously construct the efficient flow. Thus policy words are more than words, in the sense that they are performative, establishing new patterns of governance in the automobile factory. In this way, the performance of the Lean management models is linguistic, objectifying certain words, while leaving others aside, producing certain regimes of thought. Via handbooks and management consultants, these policy words are always ready to move, but what type of environment are they moving into?

## Policy words in the world of preschools

The managerial policy of the Lean management model entered a world with its own words: *pedagogical documentation, gender equality, democracy, group learning*, and *co-operation*, visible in such policy documents as the National Swedish Curriculum for Preschools (Preschool Curriculum 2011, published in English in

2011) and in the Reggio-Emilia[3] pedagogy, which was guiding most public preschools in Sweden. The Preschool Curriculum was revised in 2010 (Preschool Curriculum 2011); it comprised a 16-page policy document that was set to govern all preschools in Sweden. The Preschool Curriculum was divided into two parts, similar to the Curriculum for Schools, where the first part included the fundamental values and tasks of the preschool and the second part included the goals and guidelines. The first paragraph of the document, including the fundamental values, set the tone, emphasizing democracy, lifelong learning, human rights, individual rights, and respect for the shared environment:

> Democracy forms the foundation of the preschool. The Education Act (2010: 800) stipulates that education in the preschool aim at children acquiring and developing knowledge and values. It should promote all children's development and learning, and a lifelong desire to learn. An important task of the preschool is to impart and establish respect for human rights and the fundamental democratic values on which Swedish society is based. Each and every person working in the preschool should promote respect for the intrinsic value of each person as well as respect for our shared environment.
> 
> (Preschool Curriculum 2011: 3)

On the same page were writings about the promotion of understanding and compassion for others, aimed at establishing in children at an early age the virtues of solidarity, tolerance, non-discrimination, gender equality, and respect for differences (Preschool Curriculum 2011: 3). The following four pages of the Preschool Curriculum specified the tasks that should lay the foundation for lifelong learning and promote learning, supporting families in their role of helping children to grow and develop, giving children the opportunity to feel what it is like to overcome difficulties and feel like a valued member of a group; to develop children's trust, self-confidence, curiosity, and interest; to inspire children to explore their surroundings and develop their ability to observe and reflect. Preschools should also stimulate each child's language development and ability to communicate with different forms of expressions (Preschool Curriculum 2011: 4–7).

In the goals and guidelines section (Preschool Curriculum 2011: 8–16), the fundamental values and tasks were broken down into specific goals and guidelines regarding 'norms and values'; 'development and learning'; 'influence of the child'; 'preschool and home'; 'co-operation between the preschool class, the school and the leisure-time centre'; 'follow-up, evaluation and development'; and 'responsibility of the head of the preschool'. In the Goals and

---

3 As mentioned in Chapter 1, the Reggio-Emilia pedagogy, originally from the Reggio Emilia region of Italy, was imported to Sweden in 1992 by the Foundation of the Reggio Emilia Institute in Stockholm.

Guidelines section, most goals and guidelines pertained to 'development and learning'. Preschools should lay the foundation for learning through life (Preschool Curriculum 2011: 4). Learning was taking place in more scheduled activities, such as the Reggio-Emilia idea of the project and pedagogical documentation, which I present in greater detail in Chapters 3 and 5. But there was also a widespread idea of children's learning in play, visible in both the Curriculum and the Reggio-Emilia pedagogy. The preschool teachers were also skilled in seeing learning in play and play opportunities in learning; they introduced playing with blocks of different shapes and sizes into and as the mathematics curriculum, playing with animals into and as the natural sciences, drawing and painting into and as arts, and playing with letters into and as the language curriculum. The goals were established in the Curriculum to emphasize what preschools should strive towards to ensure the development of each child: the ability to play, for example, or to feel a sense of participation in their own culture. The Curriculum guidelines that followed were divided into the responsibility of the preschool teachers who held a university degree in preschool pedagogy (placing greater emphasis on preschools as places of pedagogy and learning), and the responsibility of the work team, which could comprise preschool teachers, teacher assistants, and non-certified teachers.

The idea of having a national Curriculum differed from the US context, for example, where preschools choose a Curriculum they consider best suited for their preschool, such as Reggio Emilia (OECD 2004) or The High/Scope Curriculum (OECD 2004). At least at the time of this study, there was a branch responsible for early childhood learning within the US Department of Education, but the actual guidelines and standards for early childhood education were set by the states. In the Massachusetts Guideline for Preschool Learning experience (Massachusetts Department of Education 2003), for example, greater emphasis was placed on the adjustment of the curriculum in relation to the specific group of children or the specific child, than was present in the Swedish Preschool Curriculum. The emphasis on choice, individualism, and self-expression were underlying values that guided the Massachusetts preschool guidelines (cf. Tobin et al. 2009), and the family was highlighted as being the primary caregiver in the guidelines (2003: 3). As Tobin et al. (2009) have noted, there is still a deep ambivalence about non-parental care in the USA that does not exist in the same way in Europe. In the Swedish Curriculum, the family and preschools should work in co-operation to ensure that children develop according to their potential (Preschool Curriculum 2011: 4), and although children should be given the opportunity to develop as individuals, there is emphasis on the ability to co-operate and become good, democratic citizens (Preschool Curriculum 2011: 3). Both the Swedish Curriculum and the Massachusetts guidelines did emphasize children's learning through play, however, along with the importance of language skills for development (Massachusetts Department of Education 2003: 3; Preschool Curriculum 2011: 6).

30  Words

The use of a national curriculum also differed from the UK context, where there was a statutory framework that set the standards for learning, development, and care; and England, Scotland, Wales, and Northern Ireland each has its own framework. In the English framework, the overarching principles that should shape early-years education from birth to the age five were: (1) 'every child is a unique child, who is constantly learning and can be resilient, capable, confident and self-assured'; (2) 'children learn to be strong and independent through positive relationships'; (3) 'children learn and develop well in enabling environments, in which their experiences respond to their individual needs and there is a strong partnership between practitioners and parents and/or carers'; and (4) 'children develop and learn in different ways and at different rates. The framework covered the education and care of all children in early-years provision, including children with special educational needs and disabilities' (Department of Education England 2017: 6). The rest of the 37-page document was about learning requirements, assessments, safeguarding, and welfare requirements, such as health and safety, staff training, skills and ratio, and special educational needs. This part of the document is relatively detailed, as is the Massachusetts Department of Education document, with sections on suitable staff and how medicine may be distributed, neither of which was present in the Swedish Curriculum. Like the Swedish and the Massachusetts documents, the English statutory framework served as a guide to preschool work and emphasized the importance of learning through play. In the English document, the ability to co-operate and play co-operatively (Department of Education England 2017) was also similar to the policy outlined in the Swedish Curriculum.

There are certain words in these documents that are typical policy words in motion, such as gender equality, democracy, human rights, and lifelong learning, that show up in many policy documents in organizations around the world. Then there are other policy words, such as co-operation, that have a particular meaning in the preschool context, in which children are taught to become co-operative citizens who value democratic processes and work well together. How is all of this played out in the preschool environment?

## Working through policy words among preschool children

In this section, the 'unplanned' activities in one of the preschools where I conducted fieldwork serve as an illustration of the way preschool teachers would interpret such everyday activities as learning and caring in relation to the policy words of the Preschool Curriculum – in this case *gender equality* and *co-operation*.

### Gender equality in the everyday experiences of preschools

Bumblebee Preschool consisted of four divisions. The division for the smallest children, approximately 1- to 2-year-olds, comprised 18 children and 4 preschool teachers. A second was for 2- to 3-year-olds, and included 22 children and 4 teachers. The third division comprised 12 3- to 4-year-olds and 2 teachers; this division — the so-called nature and culture group — spent most of its time outside of the preschool in city parks and museums. The fourth division was for the older children, between ages 4 and 6, and included 24 children and 4 preschool teachers.

It was the autumn of 2013 and I was sitting at one of the child-height tables on one of the child-height chairs in one of the rooms in the 2- to 3-year-olds' division. It was afternoon, and some of the children were still having their afternoon nap in another room, while others were up busying themselves next door. One of the preschool teachers was completing the chart for how the children had eaten and how many times they had been to the bathroom or had their diapers changed, so that parents could check when they came to pick up their children. I had been told that entering this information on the chart made room for the preschool teachers to talk to the parents about things that had happened during the day other than urination, bowel movements, and food, because the questions parents usually asked centred on those issues. Teachers were encouraged by management to talk about daily events, but they also wanted to do it. Some of the preschool teachers had also developed a real skill in portraying the events of the day, relating an episode to parents when they came to pick up their children. It was part of the Reggio-Emilia pedagogy to be able to observe and communicate children's learning to the parents.

I was sitting at a table with a group of children threading beads onto pipe cleaners. One of the children was frustrated because she was not able to communicate as she would have liked. She was nearly two years old and seemed to understand everything that was said to her, but she had not mastered the ability to use the spoken language herself. When she realized that I understood that she wanted to have a pipe cleaner to thread beads, her face lit up, and she could not stop asking for pipe cleaners and beads. Other children joined us, and at one point I had five children sitting around the table asking for pipe cleaners. I distributed pipe cleaners of every colour and made sure the children could reach the beads by putting a selection in small cups around the table. After a few days of the same scenario, one of the preschool teachers reminded me and the other teachers that we needed to make sure that the children knew there were other things that they could do. She was especially concerned with girls falling into the habit of making bracelets with golden pipe cleaners and shiny beads that were admired by children and parents. This scene had been played out several times during the last couple of days, although parents had equally admired the boys' bracelets. The teacher wanted to break the stereotypical behaviour of girls being admired for how sweet they look. According to the Swedish Preschool Curriculum, one of the fundamental policy words was gender equality. Page 4 of the Preschool Curriculum stated:

> The ways in which adults respond to girls and boys, as well as the demands and expectations imposed on children contribute to their appreciation of gender differences. The preschool should counteract traditional gender

patterns and gender roles. Girls and boys in the preschool should have the same opportunities to develop and explore their abilities and interests without having limitations imposed by stereotyped gender roles.

(Preschool Curriculum 2011: 4)

This was strong wording, and compared to the Massachusetts guidelines, it appeared even stronger. In the Massachusetts guidelines, it is instead written that preschool teachers should 'talk about the differences between boys and girls, boys/men, girls/women as questions arise' and 'talk about the constancy of gender throughout life (e.g. boys grow up to be men, girls to be women; girls will be the mommies, boys will be the daddies)' (Massachusetts Department of Education 2003: 35).

The preschool teachers took gender equality and the writings in the Curriculum seriously, as does the Swedish state, which is concerned with and fights for gender equality. The preschool teachers continuously tried to challenge themselves in this regard, and they kept a note pad in the staff restroom on which they wrote things that suggested stereotypical gender roles, to remind themselves to fight their own prejudices. On the wall in the restroom one could read such statements as 'Why is it always the mothers who call in when children are sick?'

The environment was also to serve as a *third teacher* according to the Reggio-Emilia pedagogy (Wurm 2005: 38). The division for 2- to 3-year-olds currently included six rooms with various play areas. The atelier was by far the largest room; this was where the children drew and painted; played with dough, paper, and scissors; threaded beads onto pipe cleaners; played with sand, played games; solved jigsaw puzzles with letters or numbers; or involved themselves with other pedagogical tools in one of the other play areas in the room. The second largest room also included several play areas. One was 'construction', where the children could play with blocks of different sizes, Brio railways and trains (or rather the cheaper IKEA replica), and Legos. At another play area called 'animals', children could play with small plastic animals. The 'family' play area contained stuffed animals, a small pretend stove, cups, and plates, and other items that would be included in a home.

Apart from these two main rooms, there were also two small rooms, one used for sleeping. When the children were awake, the same room could be turned into a disco or a room for playing with light and shadows. The other small room included pillows and books, where it was possible to read to the children, or for the children to pretend-read to each other. And the upper hallway contained a round carpet where the circle time was held in 2 groups of 11. This way of organizing the preschool environment is in line with the Reggio-Emilia pedagogy (see Wurm 2005: 30). Apart from these four pedagogical rooms, there was a toilet area with room to change diapers, a plastic box for each child where the parents could put extra clothes, and two small-sized toilets for the children not wearing diapers. Walking down the stairs, the 2- to 3-year-olds had room on the ground floor hallway where they kept their outerwear.

The preschool also contained communal areas such as the canteen, the wet room, and the so-called square (as in a market square). The idea of a square serving as a communal meeting space is typical of Reggio Emilia (Wurm 2005: 29). In this preschool, it was on the ground floor of the two-storey preschool – a place where children meet from different divisions to experiment with light and figures with the light-box and mirrors, construct ball tracks, or play with letters and numbers. All of this was consistent with Reggio Emilia's idea of the children's right to explore and experiment (Wurm 2005: 66). The right to explore was also emphasized in the Preschool Curriculum (2011: 5).

In this way, the play areas were organized differently than when I was a child in the 1970s. I spent most of my time in preschool in what was then called the doll room – not so much for the dolls, but for the small pretend stove, the small kitchen table, and the small dishes and cutlery and fake food. In the preschool I studied, there were no dolls or cars. What would be equivalent of a doll room was the family play area. And where there would have been cars, there were trains in a construction play area. The use of such terms as *family play area* and *construction* was an attempt to break down stereotypical gender behaviour by labelling the play areas in a way that would signal that they were meant for both girls and boys. The preschool teachers also knew that words mattered and tried to make toys gender neutral by not using terms like *legogubbe* (Lego man), but replacing it with *legofigur* (a Lego person/character). (Although, in all honesty, most Lego persons/characters represent men.) The preschool teacher worked under the assumption that words are performative, and they did attempt to break up stereotypical gender roles through language work in accordance with the Preschool Curriculum. It is through the collaborative mode of preschool teachers, the Preschool Curriculum, and the Reggio-Emilia pedagogy that preschool regimes of thought in Sweden are created and recreated.

## *Individuality in co-operation*

Another set of fundamental policy words in the Preschool Curriculum were the 'understanding and compassion for others', the 'ability to co-operate', and 'democratic values' (Preschool Curriculum 2011: 3, 5). Understanding and compassion for others and the ability to co-operate was necessary in a preschool environment, but not always a skill that the children acquired or even desired. The teachers were constantly working on these skills, especially during the 'unplanned' activities when the children could (almost) decide for themselves where they wanted to play. Breaking up fights or quarrels was part of the everyday work life of the preschool teachers. They stressed the ability to co-operate by constantly pointing out that fights were unwanted, using pedagogical tools in talking to the children – not telling them how *not* to behave, for instance, but telling them how they *should* behave. It was also important to know that the child starting the fight had apologized. The children were also taught, early on, to use the word 'stop' and/or hold out their hand to signal that they did not want to play or participate in whatever activity they were invited to. In the next chapter, I expand on the 'democratic values' and becoming a 'good citizens' in the Preschool Curriculum through the help of an illustration from the circle time, but for now I focus on the ability to co-operate and have compassion for each other.

Returning to the 2- to 3-year-old children in the atelier, one of the teachers sat down at another table and brought out clay. Soon a group of children gathered around her to play with and make things out of the clay. Other children went to construction, while a preschool teacher kept a watchful eye to ensure that they behaved, shared the toys, and played nicely together. For a while it worked well, until two of the children wanted the same block and there was need for teacher intervention. Meanwhile, one of the children was standing at the window looking at the bus that arrived at the bus stop. He managed to pique the interest of some of the other children, and they all stood in front of the window and pointed and talked about the bus. Later, they used some of the chairs to construct their own bus. But who should be the bus driver? Again a teacher had to intervene, to prevent any one child from monopolizing the position. In various instances during the day, the children were trained in the ability to co-operate and show understanding and compassion for others. All in all, the Curriculum and the Reggio-Emilia pedagogy were introduced to encourage children to become individuals, but also to learn how to co-operate in groups. Co-operation was a fundamental policy word, along with gender equality, non-discrimination, and democratic values. In other words, children should 'experience themselves as a valued member of the group' (Preschool Curriculum 2011: 5).

The regime of thought produced in preschools through the policy words of the Curriculum and the Reggio-Emilia pedagogy emphasized preschools as a place of learning, not merely to learn letters and numbers, paint, make bracelets from pipe cleaners, or build a bus out of chairs, but also how to play together, how to co-operate, to become individuals – but individuals who are able to work in groups, even to appreciate group learning. They were to develop without prejudice, unaware of gender stereotypes and other types of stereotypes. It was a certain type of citizen that was formulated in the policy documents of the Curriculum and in the Reggio-Emilia pedagogy that had little to do with the clusters of policy words and the regime of thought of the Lean management model. In the following section, I present a historical account of how Lean came to be introduced into the Swedish public preschools.

## Moving Lean policy words into Swedish public preschools

The travel of ideas and management models is a well-established research area in management studies (Czarniawska and Sevón 1996; Furusten 1999; Røvik

2000; Sahlin-Andersson and Engwall 2002; Djelic and Sahlin-Andersson 2006). I am not able to produce a genealogy of the Lean model as a proper history of management, in line with Marie-Laure Djelic's (2017) historic account of how the ATLAS organization missioned the neoliberal idea through the spreading of an organizational architecture of neoliberal think tanks. But I can point to the spread of the Lean model across industries and services by showing places and areas where Lean has appeared around the world and point to the management books, handbooks, consultants, and coaches that make it possible.

The Lean model originated in the Toyota plant (Ohno 1988), and was developed by Womack et al. (1990) as Lean production. Others, like Liker (2004) have also argued for the Toyota way and Lean management. There is a long list of industries and manufacturing companies that has introduced the Lean management model into their plants. Womack and Jones's (1996) book *Lean Thinking* describes some such industries, as exemplified by Porsche in Germany and several manufacturing companies in the USA. In *Becoming Lean*, edited by Jeffrey Liker (1997), there are examples from manufacturing companies in metal forming, plastics processing, and tooling and machining in Midwest USA (Rasch 1997), a steering gear company in Michigan (Woolson and Husar 1997), a leather tanning company in Maryland (Traynor 1997), and an automotive mirror manufacturer in Michigan (Liker and Allman 1997), among others. In his dissertation, Per-Olof Brehmer (1999) presents the introduction of Lean in one US and four European freight companies, and Zoe Radnor (2000) introduces an example from a UK chemical company. In Sweden, Scania Trucks has used Lean (Garsten et al. 2006) since the beginning of the 1990s, and Volvo has used it since 1995 (Ahlstrand 1998). In his dissertation, Per Åhlström (1997) describes an office machine company in Sweden using Lean. Lean has also been used in such services as call centres (Piercy and Rich 2009).

The fact that the Lean management model appeared in various companies around the world was helped by a number of consultancies, not least the Womack and Jones US-based Lean Enterprise Institute and their UK-based Lean Enterprise Academy. In 1996, Womack and Jones (1996) published *Lean Thinking*, in which they advocated not merely for Lean production, but for a Lean enterprise to take what they explained as the Lean leap from mass production to Lean thinking and Lean action throughout the entire enterprise. It was through this process that Lean management was turned into a model that could be moved around the world and into various industries and services. In *Lean Thinking*, Womack and Jones also introduced the idea of using Lean in healthcare.

Healthcare was the first sector to adopt Lean that dealt with humans as a product. The Lean Enterprise had been intent on eliminating waste on the production line; now humans were the items that should be moved through the hospital as efficiently as possible. In Europe, healthcare is also funded primarily by taxes, and the use of Lean was a response to political calls for efficiency, not to 'waste' taxpayers' money. Lean healthcare was introduced in some

US hospitals in 2002 (e.g. Virginia Mason Medical Center in Seattle) and in some UK hospitals in 2001, and quickly spread throughout the UK and US healthcare sector (Brandao de Souza 2009; Radnor et al. 2012). The Danish newspaper, *Berlingske Business*,[4] reported in 2008 that nowhere in the world had Lean spread into as many industries as in Denmark. Danske Bank, half of the production industry, and one-quarter of the trade-and-service business used Lean by then, and the government wanted Danish hospitals and the Migration office to join them. Numerous articles also present cases of Lean in healthcare in other parts of the world such as in Brazil (Tortorella et al. 2017) and in Senegal (Kanamori et al. 2015).

Healthcare was the first area in the Swedish public sector to introduce Lean. In 2004, Trägårdh and Lindberg (2004) presented six case studies of Lean healthcare in Sweden, and by 2011 it was reported in the *Läkartidningen*[5] (Newspaper for Medical Doctors) that nine out of ten hospitals in Sweden were using Lean. Soon after, Lean started to move into the Swedish public sector with the help of Ramboll consultancy and Lean Forum Sverige, for example. Niklas Modig and Per Åhlström (2011) helped pave the way with their book, *Vad är Lean*, which later materialized into public-sector offices and was rewritten in English as *This Is Lean* (Modig and Åhlström 2012). It was subsequently translated into Swedish and updated as *Detta är Lean* (Modig and Åhlström 2014), and now appears in Finnish and Norwegian, for example. In this way, Lean was circulated in the public sector and was introduced in such state authorities as the Swedish Migration Agency and the Swedish Council for Higher Education in 2008, the Swedish Police in 2009, the Swedish Board of Student Finance (CSN) in 2010, and the Swedish Social Insurance Agency in 2013.

A similar development occurred in Swedish municipalities, where my study of preschools also played out. Sweden comprises 290 municipalities that govern their own schools, preschools, social services, homecare, and care of the elderly; they are responsible for providing a significant proportion of the everyday public services used by citizens. Municipal public services are financed by taxes, even if the operator is a private company. All taxable people in Sweden pay taxes to the municipality (and the region – the region of Stockholm, for example). As of 2018, only people with an annual income exceeding 455,300 SEK (~ 45,530 EUR; ~ 53,900 USD) pay taxes to the state, which finances such state authorities as the Swedish police. Municipalities have independent power of taxation and municipal taxes vary, but the average municipal rate is approximately 15–20 per cent and the regional tax is 10–15 per cent.[6]

---

4 'Danmark på vej at blive et Lean-samfund' by Vibeke Lyngklip Svansø, 21 September 2008.
5 *Läkartidningen* no. 39, vol 108, 2011.
6 In 2018, taxes in the Municipality of Stockholm were 17.90 per cent and taxes in the Region of Stockholm were 12.08 per cent.

The independence of municipalities also means that municipalities determine how they want to run their organization, which includes the introduction of management models, such as Lean. According to Chapter 4 of the Education Act, however, they cannot choose not to have any so-called systematic quality work. And because management models such as Lean promise continuous improvement and enhancement of quality, it made sense for them to adopt Lean. Lean has been launched in many municipalities in Sweden. The following list is far from exhaustive, and is presented here merely to provide an idea of the rapid spread of Lean in Swedish municipalities:

| | | |
|---|---|---|
| Stockholm Region | Solna | 2007 |
| | Södertälje and Järfälla | 2008 |
| | Some districts in Stockholm City | 2009 |
| West of Sweden | Halmstad | 2007 |
| | Falkenberg and Kungsbacka | 2009 |
| | Varberg | 2010 |
| | Hylte | 2013 |
| | Kils | 2016 |
| South of Sweden | Malmö | 2008 |
| | Bromölla | 2010 |
| North of Sweden | Sundsvall | 2010 |
| | Åre | 2016 |

In the Swedish municipality where I did my fieldwork, Lean was introduced as a way of making public services more efficient, hence more qualitative, and thereby having co-workers feel more 'joy at work'. All services in the municipality were included: social work, homecare, care for the elderly, and preschools, for example. The idea in preschools was to become more efficient, so that teachers would have more time with the children. In the municipality, management had developed a way of organizing the Lean reform by employing a so-called development strategist to initiate and establish the reform over five years. She was in charge of organizing the Lean work by ensuring that management and employees learnt about Lean and its uses and by supporting the unit heads in their decisions about the need for applying a Lean tool and which tool would be helpful in making the necessary improvements. The development strategist's key task was to guarantee that there were enough Lean coaches in the organization. If a unit head experienced a problem that the development strategist and the unit head agreed could be solved by a Lean tool, then Lean coaches, often in pairs, were sent to the unit to work with a group of unit employees in *improvement groups* to solve the problem. The Lean coaches were administrators, social workers, homecare workers, workers caring for the elderly and disabled, and preschool teachers in the municipality. These employees had expressed an interest in being part of the municipality's investment in making the municipality a Lean organization, and they spent part of their working hours as Lean coaches in the municipality. These Lean coaches had received their Lean training from consultants, and were set to turn the entire municipality Lean. The Lean coaches met in the municipalities' Lean Forum around six times a year to discuss how to train staff to be Lean and to continue their own Lean education.

The packaging of Lean policy words into immutable management books, handbooks by Lean gurus like James P. Womack and Daniel T. Jones, Jeffrey K. Liker, or in the Swedish case, Niklas Modig and Per Åhlström, is part of the process of making the model mobile. The language work performed by Lean gurus, consultants, and the media make the spreading of the model possible. In the municipality studied here, Lean coaches furthered the language work by introducing Lean policy words into public services. Via handbooks, management consultants and Lean coaches, the Lean policy words moved into new environments. In this collaborative mode, the Lean clusters of policy words performed in preschools introduced Lean regimes of thought.

## Conclusion: in the name of efficiency

Policy words are often recognizable from other domains, used in other policies: 'Gender equality' has its own policy field and 'continuous improvement' is part of Total Quality Management, for example. In this way, the preschool policy documents and the Lean management model tap into pre-existing ideas of the nature of a good citizen or an efficient manager. The universalism of these policy words is, in many ways, a prerequisite for the Lean management model to operate in different types of organizations. Still, it is the choice of words, independently and collectively, that reveal the regimes of thought embedded in preschool policy documents and the Lean management models. Lean policy words have a specific meaning and project value in the preschool context. Semantic clusters of policy words have a 'thing-ified quality' (Urla 2012) that make them immutable and moveable. They are imbued with values that turn the focus towards efficiency, creating new environments of power and new patterns of governance in preschools.

The Swedish municipalities have in common that most of their public services centre around caring for and educating people, while considering such policies as gender equality, democratic values, human rights, non-discrimination, and respect for differences. And in the schools and preschools, teachers must also teach such skills as the ability to co-operate and engage in gender equality, integrating these skills into their teaching of letters, mathematics, natural sciences, and their encouragement of lifelong learning. The semantic clusters of policy words in the Preschool Curriculum are geared towards the fostering of good, well-educated citizens, whereas clusters of Lean policy words are geared towards the delivery of an efficient product or service promoting smooth-flowing performance, eliminating waste, and providing continuous improvement.

Lean policy words create a Lean language with specific wording that points the preschool teachers in a specific direction. It is the performative collaborative mode – how Lean policy words, through their objectified quality, interact with the preschool world, which are part of turning the Lean management model into an empirical fact in preschools. How this is played out will be shown in the chapters to come.

## References

Ahlstrand, Roland (1998), *En tid av förändring: dominerande koalitioner och organisationsstrukturer vid Volvo lastvagnars monteringsfabriker i Tuve 1982–1994* (Lund: Department of Sociology, Lund University).

Åhlström, Pär (1997), *Sequences in the process of adopting Lean production* (Stockholm: Economic Research Institute, Stockholm School of Economics).

Austin, John Langshaw (1962), *How to do things with words* (Cambridge, MA: Harvard University Press).

Brandao de Souza, Luciano (2009), 'Trends and approaches in Lean healthcare', *Leadership in Health Services*, 22 (2), 121–139.

Brehmer, Per-Olof (1999), *Towards a model of Lean freight transport operations* (Linköping: Linköpings University, Department of Management and Economics).

Callon, Michel (1995), 'Four models for the dynamics of science', in G.E. Markle, S. Jasanoff, J.C. Petersen, and T.J. Pinch (ed.), *Thousand Oaks* (Thousand Oaks: Sage), 29–63.

——— (1998), 'Introduction: The embeddedness of economic markets in economics', in Michel Callon (ed.), *The laws of the markets* (Oxford: Blackwell), 1–57.

Czarniawska, Barbara and Sevón, Guje (eds.) (1996), *Translating organizational change* (Berlin: Walter de Gruyter).

Department of Education England (2017), *Statutory framework for the early years foundation stage: Setting the standards for learning, development and care for children from birth to five [England]* (United Kingdom: Crown copyright).

Djelic, Marie-Laure (2017), 'Building an architecture for political influence: Atlas and the transnational institutionalization of the neoliberal think tank', in Christina Garsten and Adrienne Sörbom (eds.), *Power, policy and profit: Corporate engagement in politics and governance* (Cheltenham: Edward Elgar), 1–25.

Djelic, Marie-Laure and Sahlin-Andersson, Kerstin (2006), *Transnational governance: Institutional dynamics of regulation* (Cambridge: Cambridge University Press).

Duchêne, Alexandre and Heller, Monica (eds.) (2012), *Language in late capitalism: Pride and profit* (New York: Routledge).

Foucault, Michel (1988), 'The political technology of individuals', in Luther H. Martin, Huch Gutman, and Patrick H. Hutton (eds.), *Technologies of the self: A seminar with Michel Foucault* (Amherst, MA: University of Massachusetts Press).

——— (1991), 'Governmentality', in Graham Burchell, Colin Gordon, and Peter Miller (eds.), *The Foucault effect: Studies in governmentality* (Chicago: University of Chicago Press).

Furusten, Staffan (1999), *Popular management books: How they are made and what they mean for organisations* (London: Routledge).

Gallie, Walter Bryce (1955), 'Essentially contested concepts', *Proceedings of the Aristotelian Society*, 56, 167–198.

Garsten, Christina, Lindvert, Jessica, Jambrén, Niklas and Thedvall, Renita. (2006), 'From employment to the development of workers' capabilities: Mobility, learning and responsibility in Swedish worklife', (Report for the European Commission).

Gluck, Carol and Tsing, Anna Lowenhaupt (2009), *Words in motion: Toward a global lexicon* (Durham: Duke University Press).

Harvey, David (1990), *The condition of postmodernity: An enquiry into the origins of cultural change* (Oxford: Blackwell).

Heller, Monica (2010), 'The commodification of language', *Annual Review of Anthropology*, 39 (1), 101–114.

Holmes, Douglas R. (2009), 'Economy of words', *Cultural Anthropology*, 24 (3), 381–419.

────── (2014), *Economy of words: Communicative imperatives in central banks* (Chicago: University of Chicago Press).

İslamoğlu, Huri (2009), 'Komisyon/Commission and Kurul/Board: Words that rule', in Carol Gluck and Anna Lowenhaupt Tsing (eds.), *Words in motion, toward a global lexicon* (Durham: Duke University Press), 265–285.

James, Allison (2012), 'Child-centredness' and "the child": The cultural politics of nursery schooling in England', in Anne Trine Kjørholt and Jens Qvortrup (eds.), *The modern child and the flexible labour market: Early childhood education and care* (New York: Palgrave Macmillan), 111–127.

Kanamori, Shogo, Sow, Seydou, Castro, Marcia C., Matsuno, Rui, Tsuru, Akiko and Jimba, Masamine (2015), 'Implementation of 5S management method for Lean healthcare at a health center in Senegal: A qualitative study of staff perception', *Glob Health Action*, 8, 27256.

Latour, Bruno (1986), 'Visualisation and cognition: Drawing things together', in Henrika Kuklick and Elizabeth Long (eds.), *Knowledge and society: Studies in the sociology of culture past and present* (6; Greenwich, CT: JAI Press).

Li, Tania Murray (2007), *The will to improve: Governmentality, development, and the practice of politics* (Durham: Duke University Press).

Liker, Jeffrey K. (1997), *Becoming Lean: Inside stories of US manufacturers* (Portland: Productivity Press).

────── (2004), *The Toyota way: 14 management principles from the world's greatest manufacturer* (London: McGraw-Hill).

Liker, Jeffrey K. and Allman, Keith (1997), 'The Donnelly production system: Lean at grand haven', in Jeffrey K. Liker (ed.), *Becoming Lean: Inside stories of US manufacturers* (Portland: Productivity Press), 201–246.

Martin, Emily (1997), 'Managing Americans', in Cris Shore and Susan Wright (eds.), *Anthropology of policy: Perspectives on governance and power* (London: Routledge), 183.

Massachusetts Department of Education (2003), *Guidelines for Preschool learning experiences* (Malden, MA: Early Childhood Advisory Council to the Massachusetts Board of Education).

Modig, Niklas and Åhlström, Per (2011), *Vad är Lean? En guide till kundfokus och flödeseffektivitet* (Stockholm: Stockholm School of Economics Institute for Research).

────── (2012), *This is Lean: Resolving the efficiency paradox* (Stockholm: Rheologica Publishing).

────── (2014), *Detta är Lean. Lösningen på effektivitetsparadoxen* (Stockholm: Rheologica Publishing).

Oakes, Leslie S., Townley, Barbara, and Cooper, David J. (1998), 'Business planning as pedagogy: Language and control in a changing institutional field', *Administrative Science Quarterly*, 43, 257–292.

OECD (2004), *Starting strong: Curricula and pedagogies in early education and care* (Paris: Directorate for Education, OECD).
Ohno, Taiichi (1988), *Toyota production system: Beyond large-scale production* (London: CRC Press).
Piercy, Niall and Rich, Nick (2009), 'Lean transformation in the pure service environment: The case of the call service centre', *International Journal of Operations & Production Management*, 29 (1), 54–76.
Preschool Curriculum (2011), 'Curriculum for the Preschool Lpfö 98 revised 2010', in Skolverket (Swedish National Agency for Education) (ed.) (Stockholm).
Radnor, Zoe J. (2000), 'Changing to a Lean organisation: The case of a chemicals company', *International Journal of Manufacturing Technology and Management*, 1 (4–5), 444–454.
Radnor, Zoe J., Holweg, Matthias, and Waring, Justin (2012), 'Lean in healthcare: The unfilled promise?', *Social Science & Medicine*, 74 (3), 364–371.
Rasch, Steven F. (1997), 'Lean manufacturing practices at small and medium-sized US parts suppliers-does it work?', in Jeffrey K. Liker (ed.), *Becoming Lean: Inside stories of US manufacturers* (Portland: Productivity Press), 103–118.
Rose, Nicolas (1992), 'Governing the enterprising self', in Paul Heelas and Paul Morris (eds.), *The values of enterprising culture: The moral debate* (London: Routledge).
Røvik, Kjell Arne (2000), *Moderna organisationer: Trender inom organisationstänkandet vid millennieskiftet* (Malmö: Liber).
Sahlin-Andersson, Kerstin and Engwall, Lars (2002), *The expansion of management knowledge: Carriers, flows and sources* (Stanford: Stanford University Press).
Shankar, Shalini and Cavanaugh, Jillian R. (2012), 'Language and materiality in global capitalism', *Annual Review of Anthropology*, 41 (1), 355–369.
Shore, Cris and Wright, Susan (1997), *Anthropology of policy: Perspectives on governance and power* (London: Routledge).
Silverstein, Michael (1996), 'Monoglot "standard" in America: Standardization and metaphors of linguistic hegemony', in Michael Silverstein, Donald Brenneis, and Ronald K.S. Macaulay (eds.), *The matrix of language: Contemporary linguistic anthropology* (Boulder, CO: Westview Press).
Tamm Hallström, Kristina and Thedvall, Renita (2015), 'Managing administrative reform through language work: Implementing Lean in Swedish public sector organisations', *Scandinavian Journal of Public Administration*, 19 (2), 89–108.
Taylor, Frederick Winslow (1911 [2006]), *The principles of scientific management* (Middlesex: The Echo Library).
Tobin, Joseph, Hsueh, Yeh, and Karasawa, Mayumi (2009), *Preschool in three cultures revisited: China, Japan, and the United States* (Chicago: University of Chicago Press).
Tortorella, Guilherme Luz, Fogliatto, Flávio Sanson, Anzanello, Michel, Marodin, Giuliano Almeida, Garcia, Mayara, and Reis Esteves, Rafael (2017), 'Making the value flow: Application of value stream mapping in a Brazilian public healthcare organisation', *Total Quality Management & Business Excellence*, 28 (13–14), 1544–1558.
Trägårdh, Björn and Lindberg, Kajsa (2004), 'Curing a meagre health care system by Lean methods: Translating "chains of care" in the Swedish health care sector', *The International Journal of Health Planning and Management*, 19 (4), 383–398.
Traynor, Sean G. (1997), 'Making leather leaner: The garden state tanning story', in Jeffrey K. Liker (ed.), *Becoming Lean: Inside stories of US manufacturers* (Portland: Productivity Press).

Urciuoli, Bonnie and LaDousa, Chaise (2013), 'Language management/labor', *Annual Review of Anthropology*, 42 (1), 175–190.

Urla, Jacqueline (2012), 'Total quality language revival', in Monica Heller and Duchêne (eds.), *Language in late capitalism: Pride and profit* (New York: Routledge), 73–92.

Williams, Raymond (1976), *Keywords: A vocabulary of culture and society* (Oxford: Oxford University Press).

Womack, James P. and Jones, Daniel T. (1996), *Lean thinking: Banish waster and create wealth in your corporation* (New York: Simon & Schuster).

Womack, James P., Jones, Daniel T., and Roos, Daniel (1990), *Machine that changed the world: How Lean production revolutionized the global car wars* (New York: Simon & Schuster).

Woolson, Daniel and Husar, M. (1997), 'Transforming a plant to Lean in a large, traditional company: Delphi Saginaw Steering Systems, GM', in Jeffrey K. Liker (ed.), *Becoming Lean: Inside stories of US manufacturers* (Portland: Productivity Press), 121–157.

Wurm, Julianne (2005), *Working in the Reggio way: A beginner's guide for American teachers* (St. Paul, Minnesota: Redleaf Press).

# Chapter 3

# Meetings

## Lean meetings and preschool circle time

I had just observed a meeting of the preschool heads of the four preschools in Birch Preschool Unit, and Unit Head Christina asked me if I had discovered anything. I was a few weeks into my participant observation as a staff member in Birch Unit's Bumblebee Preschool and already had some impressions. I told her that I couldn't help but notice that they were struggling; two people were on part-time, long-term sick leave, two staff members were going to school once a week, and their substitutes were not really able to shoulder the responsibility. On top of that, the usual number of people was on sick leave or away at meetings, making it extra difficult to run the preschool in the way the teachers wanted it to run.

Unit Head Christina said that she had been thinking that perhaps they shouldn't have as many meetings, and that she looked forward to hearing what I had to say: 'Our idea is that it's a good way to keep us informed. It's a good way to evolve', she said. I was trying to think ahead: 'What should I say that wouldn't be misinterpreted?' I assumed that the preschool teachers would want to keep meeting in the pedagogical seminar to discuss pedagogy and that they would want to maintain their weekly planning meetings. What meetings would be eliminated? It seemed obvious to me that the solution would be more teachers, but that was unrealistic, given the current budget for preschool activities within the municipality. The municipality's solution was to bring in a management model to see if time could be made up through the organization of work, which would leave more time for the children. It was an understandable solution. If there were no budget for more teachers, then the solution might have been found by increasing the efficiency of current staff.

But what meetings were currently being held in the preschool environment, and how did they relate to Lean and Lean meetings?

The focus of this chapter is on the meeting as a practice of performing policy. The meeting is a place for practicing policy, but the meeting itself also practices policy in the way in which it is organized, the instruments used, and the material artefacts included and produced. In this way, the meeting not only makes policy, but also makes policy subjects and policy environments.

I am using the analytical framework developed by Sandler and me (Sandler and Thedvall 2017) for analysing the preschool meetings and Lean meetings. Sandler and I understand meetings in terms of 'architecture', 'practices of circulation', and 'makers'. Meetings as architectural constructs constrain and enable, and they structure and configure policy practices, documents, words, decision-making processes, and subjects and subjectivities. Practices of circulation allude to the fact that there are things going on in meetings, but that meetings are not simply the containers through which these things move; they are themselves practices of circulation, whereby policy takes form and policy is worked out. Meetings also operate as makers of governance and management. Meetings are both the architecture and the architect. Irrespective of intention, meetings make certain processes possible and close the door to other directions of development.

This chapter begins with the way Lean meetings are used in the automotive industry. I then turn to circle-time meetings in preschools, first, among 1- to 2-year-old children and then among 4- to 6-year-olds. Although most Swedish public preschools are separated into divisions, not all are divided by age, as was Bumblebee Preschool. Children in some preschools are placed in what is referred to as sibling groups, which may comprise children from one to six. I present ethnographic material from the circle-time meeting, which shows the making of democratic citizens. In the next section, I portray a pedagogical reflection meeting, at which the preschool teachers reflect and analyse so-called pedagogical documentation, as one of the key tools for organizing pedagogical work in the preschool. In the final part of the chapter, I focus on a preschool management meeting, at which the preschool heads of Birch Preschool Unit were set to turn their preschool information boards (a whiteboard) into a Lean board (a whiteboard), enabling Lean staff meetings. In the conclusion, I advance the notion that meetings, through their architecture, organization, and material artefacts, concentrate not only a particular issue; rather, they serve as a force turned into a powerful package with the power to change directions.

## Meetings as events-that-model

A management model meeting functions as an 'event-that-models' (Handelman 1990 [1998]). Handelman, who is interested in events in relation to ritual, writes about the event-that-models the lived-in world and the event-that-presents the lived-in world. He argues that there are two types of events: those that model society and those that mirror society. Those that model society are specialized, relatively closed systems that have a high degree of autonomy from the lived-in world (Handelman 1990 [1998]). Those events-that-present, on the other hand, are representational, mirroring social order in modern society. A management model like Lean has an event-like character as an event-that-models, in the sense that much of the Lean work is performed as events in Lean meetings. It is through these meetings that the Lean model as an 'immutable mobile' (Latour 1986) is played out, including specific policy words, technologies, and actors (actants); and it is through the meeting that it becomes an event-that-models. It may not be the modelling anticipated by the preschool teachers or even the future promised by the model, but it means and does things in the preschools.

Ethnographic studies in and of meetings have seen a revival in recent years in anthropological writing and other social sciences. (For a more detailed account, see Sandler and Thedvall [2017].) My own interest in 'meeting ethnography' (Sandler and Thedvall 2017) is based on doing ethnography in meetings in relation to my dissertation work in the European Commission and following the work of various European Union Committees and working groups (Thedvall 2005, 2006, 2008, 2013). When I was writing my dissertation in the beginning of the 2000s, the array of articles on meetings available today did not exist. I found my way with the help of Helen B. Schwartzman's (1989) *The Meeting* – a classic among scholars in the area. Through Schwartzman, I discovered such early ethnographers as Audrey Richards and Adam Kuper (1971) and F.G. Bailey (1965), who were interested in meetings. And Fred Myers (1986), who wrote about speech at meetings among the Australian Pintupi, and how meetings worked as mediators between two central values: relatedness and autonomy. And Don Brenneis and Myers (1984), who argued that speech events, like meetings, make power possible. Brenneis (1994, 2009) later focused on the construction of social scientific knowledge through peer review and academic meeting settings in the US National Research Council, which he saw as reading events 'at the intersection of text and talk', characteristic of bureaucratic discourse. Apart from the anthropological writing, I was also inspired by the work of sociologist Erving Goffman (1959, 1963 [1966]) on meetings as social gatherings with a central situational focus, Deidre Boden's (1994) work on the business of talk in organizations, and van Vree's (1999) work on the history of the modern meeting.

When Jen Sandler and I (Sandler and Thedvall 2017) started discussing meetings, we returned to Schwartzman's book, *The Meeting*, and began thinking of meetings as a technology. We then took a tour through the infrastructure literature within anthropology (Larkin 2013), which brought about the notions of 'architecture' and 'practice of circulation'. Infrastructure enabled us to maintain within the concept of the meeting a notion of the formal, replicable, invisible structuring elements and the practices of circulation of ideas, instruments, and documents. In the end, though, the concept of infrastructure seemed to hide what we were trying to get at. Instead of considering the meeting as infrastructure, we used the notions of the 'architecture' and 'practices of circulation', and forewent the overarching concept of infrastructure. We then added a third dimension: the meeting as a 'maker' of governance and management.

When doing research on the Lean management model in preschools, I had reason to return to meeting ethnography and the literature on meetings, because work with Lean is in many ways played out in meetings (Thedvall

2017) – but not only work with Lean. There are other activities that use the meeting as a maker of policy subjects and policy environments, such as preschool circle time, pedagogical reflection meetings, and preschool management meetings.

## The meetings of management models

It is easy to find management literature that celebrates the meeting as a way of improving business: improvement-group meetings or board meetings (a whiteboard), as suggested by Lean (Womack et al. 1990), quality improvement teams or problem-solving teams in Total Quality Management (Deming 1986), or team learning in the Learning Organization (Senge 1994 [2006]). The *board meeting* is central to Lean. The Lean board meeting has a particular aesthetic in that it should be a short – meaning efficient – stand-up meeting, wherein people stand in front of a board (often a whiteboard) rather than getting comfortable sitting and spending too much time contemplating. The managers and other employees go through what is on the board, sometimes once a week, sometimes every day. Lean board meetings should include the entire staff, guided by the idea that everyone can and wants to contribute towards improving the efficiency of work processes, and if they are not included, they will not feel responsible to do so.

The Lean board is used as a visual management technique in two ways: through the improvement board and the performance management board. The *improvement board* is a way of visualizing the people responsible for a particular improvement and where they are in the improvement process. The *performance management board* should include goals that can be evaluated and controlled; it should set targets on the assembly line and then monitor and evaluate them, rendering visual the progress of these targets. The performance management board focuses primarily on efficiency, on fast flows showing better performance. If the goal is not reached, there is room for new improvements, which moves the problem to the improvement board.

A typical performance management board in an automobile factory focuses on setting targets for the number of automobiles that should be produced. These targets are made visual and their status is tracked by green, yellow, and red symbols, where green signifies that the target has been met, yellow is a warning that the production is starting to fall behind, red indicates that the production is failing the target. The green, red, or yellow dot is generally put on the board, which is often centrally placed on the factory floor where staff meet, often before every shift begins going through what has been working and what has not. If the status is yellow or red, it indicates a need for improvement, and staff members are encouraged to come forward with suggestions or to volunteer to take part in an *improvement-group meeting* to generate solutions.

Areas in need of improvements in efficiency are then put on the improvement board, and a group of employees are set to improve it. The group meets in an improvement-group meeting and using various Lean tools they attempt to eradicate the so-called wastes that caused them to fall short of their target. Any wasteful moments should be eliminated, and employees are to write action plans on what needs to be changed. The next step in the process is for a group of employees – preferably another group of employees, in order to involve all employees – to meet and decide what actions need to be taken to deliver according to the action plans produced by the improvement group.

The architecture of the Lean meetings is centred on Lean boards. It is through the Lean board that performance is visualized and areas in need of improvement are brought to the fore. When further Lean work is needed, a group of employees in the industry is chosen to identify the various types of waste and to create action plans. It is in the improvement-group meetings and the board meetings that the Lean model is practiced. Through the Lean policy words in these meetings, the Lean regime of thought is practiced and circulated through the use of action plan documents. In this way, the Lean meetings are making Lean in the organization, pushing for flow efficiency and the elimination of waste. In preschools, meetings are practiced in other ways and based on other policies. The following two sections focus on preschool meetings: circle-time meetings with the children and pedagogical reflection meetings with preschool teachers.

## Making good, democratic citizens during circle time

It was circle time and one of the preschool teachers sat down in the circle, while the other teacher gathered all the children into the circle. Beginning the day officially with circle time is a common practice in preschools, not merely in Sweden, but also as shown in, e.g. the Tobin et al. (2009) study of Hawaiian preschools. A variation of circle time was also used in Japanese preschools, where children begin the day seated on chairs at tables facing the teacher (Ben-Ari 1997 [2013]; Tobin et al. 2009).

On this day in the autumn of 2013, I was with the group of 1- to 2-year-olds at Bumblebee Preschool. We were seated in a circle on the floor in one of the rooms in the preschool. There were dots on the floor to provide guidance for where one could sit and how big the circle was intended to be. There were 18 children and 4 teachers in the division. Some of the older children in the group knew what to do, and they sat beside the teachers; others needed to be taught the process. Some of the children wanted to sit in the lap of one of the teachers, and others comfortably took their places in the circle. Some of the children needed extra attention if they were going to sit still during circle time and needed to sit close to one of the teachers. After some time, everyone was seated, and circle time began. The circle was a policy instrument; it ensured that everyone could see, but also impregnated the notion that everyone should see and take part on equal terms. In this way, the architecture of the circle-time meeting projected ideas and values about equality.

One of the teachers had brought out a basket of rag dolls – handmade dolls that the parents had made for their child. (The preschool teachers also had their own dolls.) Parents were supplied with two body-shaped cloths that they had stitched together and filled with wadding. They were to give the doll hair and clothes, to make it resemble their child. A child with blond hair should have a doll with blond hair and a child with brown eyes should have a doll with brown eyes, though this guidance was not followed to the letter by all parents. Still, the children knew their own doll. Two-year-old Carl was responsible for circle time that day – a task that circulated among the children. The older children, like Carl, knew what to do, but the younger children needed the help of the teachers or other children. Carl took out the dolls one by one. He knew which doll belonged to which child; sometimes he tried to show the children the dolls that belonged to them – sometimes a bit too eagerly – and sometimes children would try to get his attention to claim their doll. Carl placed the doll in front of or handed the doll to the child. Some of the children became excited when they received their doll. They smiled and held it up, showing it to everyone. Others were more reserved and sat holding their doll or set it on the floor. The distribution of the dolls was a way of taking attendance with children who did not yet master spoken language. To take attendance was part of the first steps in following the rules of circle time, and eventually, when the children were older, the rules of school. In this way, circle times had several pedagogical elements, such as equality through the architecture; the ability to sit still; and an awareness of the importance of being there, of attending.

If someone was away sick or on holiday, that child's doll was placed back in the basket and one of the preschool teachers explained why the child was not present. After we were finished with the dolls, we went around the circle singing the familiar name song, in which the names of the people in the circle are inserted in turn.

> Renita is here, Pelle (being the person sitting next to me) is here, how happy we are that Lisa is here today, and in our happy gang Carl is here, how happy we are that Olivia is here today [and so on, until we had gone around the circle].

When attendance had been taken and the name song had been sung, one of the preschool teachers gave Carl a box of cards, each with a picture symbolizing a song. Carl picked one card with an owl in a tree, and the teachers and some of the children who could speak and knew the song started singing and doing movements, holding their arms up in the air, swinging them slowly as if they were trees moving in the wind:

> I'm a tree, I'm a tree, I'm a hollow tree.
> I'm a tree, I'm a tree.
> There is an owl living inside me.
> Ao ao, Ao ao, Aoao ho ho ho, Ao ao, Ao ao, Aoao ho ho ho.

All the children tried to make the movements, holding their arms up in the air. Then in the second verse, they formed their hands into a circle and held them in front of their eyes to represent an owl. When the song finished, all the children started clapping their hands. Carl picked a new card. It was a picture of a bus. Some of the children shouted happily. This was a popular song.

> The wheels on the bus go round and round,
> Round and round, round and round.
> The wheels on the bus go round and round.
> All 'round the town.

We sang the first verse while doing the movements, holding our arms at 90-degree angles and moving them in circles as if we were moving forward, and when we came to 'All 'round the town', we stretched one of our arms forward, moving from one side to the other, while pointing.

When we had finished the song, and the clapping had died down, the dolls were collected and put in the basket, and circle time was finished for the day.

Circle time among 1- to 2-year-olds was the beginning of turning the children into group members who were able to sit still in a circle and do something together. It was preparation for school, but it was also one piece in the goal of turning them into good citizens who were learning to co-operate and to participate as a group, while learning to accept and respect the individual choices of their friends (Preschool Curriculum 2011). Olwig (2011) discusses circle time in Danish preschools as part of the preschool's civilizing project of children, following Norbert Elias's theory of civilization.

The ability to accept and respect the choices of their friends and learning to co-operate was emphasized even more among the older children. One of the teachers informed the children in the 4- to 6-year-old division, which comprised 24 children and 4 preschool teachers, that it was circle time. It was Monday assembly, when the division decides what to do during the rest of the week. It took a while before all the children were seated. Some of the children sat down immediately, while others lingered, trying to avoid the assembly all together. Gustav and Jonathan needed to be separated; otherwise there would be too much kidding around and disturbing the assembly. Each week two children were designated child pedagogues, and 5-year-old Emma and Erik were the child pedagogues who were fulfilling one of their duties: holding the Monday circle-time meeting. They took their job seriously, standing beside a board, while the other children sat in the circle. The board was divided into five squares on the wall – one for each weekday. Above the taped squares was a sign that read 'Weekly meeting', and a number of activities written on pieces of laminated paper were attached to the appropriate day. Although the teachers often had a prearranged schedule, there was some leeway, with the children helping to make choices. Emma and Erik started by taking attendance, and then went through each day of the week. Of particular interest were Wednesday and Thursday – the project and excursion days. The children were divided into two groups, 12 to a group, with two teachers in each group. One of the groups was at the preschool working on their project for the term, while the other group was out on an excursion.

When I was doing my fieldwork, the children did a project with sand. Each child had brought a box of sand (easily found in Sweden) to the preschool, and part of the project was for each child in the 4- to 6-year-old group to show on a map where they had found the sand and tell the others about the sand. The sand was also sent around among the children and they felt and commented on it. All these conversations were documented in a process called pedagogical documentation, which I discuss in greater detail in the next section.

During the assembly, the children were encouraged to generate suggestions for where they could go on an excursion. Sometimes the preschool teachers tried to suggest new places; otherwise the children tended to want to go to places they were already familiar with. When they had a number of suggestions, they voted on where to go by raising their arms. It was decided that day that they would go to a nearby playground. The circle-time meeting ended with the child pedagogues choosing songs that the group would sing together. In this way, there were several practices circulating during circle time, centred on the board with a schedule for the week, where they wrote down what to do. The children took attendance, came up with possible places for their excursion, voted, and sang songs.

If circle time in preschool was about learning democratic processes and learning how to participate and collaborate in groups, Lean meetings had other issues that had to be brought to the fore. The architecture of circle time is not a stand-up meeting with a focus on efficiency and quickness, like the Lean board meeting, but a meeting at which children sit in a circle on the floor so that every child can see every other child. To see each other was the focus of the meeting – not seeing the board, as in a Lean meeting. It was at the circle-time meetings that the children learnt how to work and behave together in a group, to be able to listen to others and reflect together, and to be able to conform to majority decisions. It was practiced and circulated through the use of songs, planning, attendance, voting, and presentation of projects. In this way, the circle-time meetings trained the children how to become co-operating, democratic citizens.

## Working through pedagogical reflection meetings

One of the guidelines under the last heading of the Preschool Curriculum (2011) stated that each child's learning and development should be systematically documented, and that the ways in which the child's learning changed over time should also be documented (Preschool Curriculum 2011: 14–15). The preschools where I did fieldwork, like many of the public preschools, accounted for the children's progress by *pedagogical documentation* – the most important tool for organizing the pedagogical work at the preschools. Many public preschools in Sweden were Reggio Emilia inspired, and pedagogical documentation is a key educational tool in the Reggio-Emilia pedagogy. Assessment through pedagogical documentation does not focus so much on individual children as it does on the progression of the group, indicating the quality of preschool in general (Lillvist and Sandberg 2018). Each year, the preschool unit heads, together with their preschool heads, write a report based on the preschools' pedagogical documentation. The report is sent to the municipal preschool director and the unit head and the preschool heads are called to a meeting to discuss the report with the preschool director. I joined Birch Preschool Unit for one of these meetings, and it was a relatively informal affair, at which the preschool director asked questions and they discussed some of the areas that the unit head had identified as areas for improvement. The Swedish Schools Inspectorate regularly assesses all public and private preschools as well, based on site visits, self-reporting, a survey, and interviews with teachers and parents.

In comparison, the English system of assessment is focused on the individual child assessing the learning goals identified in the Statutory Framework for the Early Years (Department of Education England 2017) according to a 1–3 scale where the child needs to have at least a 2 to be understood as having received a 'good level of development' (Basford and Wood 2018). These assessments are used as summative assessments to serve the purpose of accountability. The Office for Standards and Education collects the data, and the summative data of a preschool are used to signify the quality and effectiveness of preschool education (Basford and Wood 2018).

To do pedagogical documentation, the teachers first observed and documented – much like an ethnographer taking field notes – how the children reacted and interacted around a specific theme – sand, water, stones, or a book they liked, for example. When my son was two, he brought his favourite book to the preschool and presented it during circle time. The teachers documented, among other things, how he showed the other children how they should knock on the doors portrayed on the pages before turning to the next page of the book. (My son was not part of my fieldwork site, but pedagogical documentation is a common tool to use in Swedish public preschools and as I received the pedagogical documentation of his presentation as parent, I have incorporated it here.)

The teachers then translated their field notes, focusing on a particular instance into a presentation – an instance that represented the theme agreed upon beforehand. The presentation in the form of pictures and/or text was then shown to the children during circle time – a picture of my son showing the other children how to knock on the page, for example. During this reflection, the preschool teachers also documented how the children reacted to and interacted with the presentation. The teachers then reflected on, analysed, and interpreted the original observation and the children's reflections in the teachers' *pedagogical reflection meetings*, in relation to particular themes related to the Curriculum, such as gender, social interaction, mathematics, pedagogical environment, language and communication, and the children's possibility of exerting influence. According to Reggio Emilia, it could be labelled pedagogical documentation only after it had been reflected upon, analysed, and interpreted by both children and teachers (and, if possible, by parents).

At pedagogical reflection meetings, preschool teachers in the role of *project carriers* presented a project they were doing at the preschool as part of their pedagogical documentation. The project carriers, usually two preschool teachers working with a children's group on a particular project, screened a film or presented photographs they had taken. The group then reflected on what they had been shown, describing what they saw, making suggestions for any improvement they considered necessary, and discussed anything that they brought with them back to their own projects.

It was in the autumn of 2013 and Astrid and Lars were the project carriers that day. Astrid (Lars was out sick) would present a project that she and Lars were doing with the 1- to 2-year-olds. Sigrid was the 'focus holder', keeping time. Astrid started to explain that she was working with the youngest children, and that they had had a summer assignment. The parents had been given the assignment of filming their children in motion for no more than 20–30 seconds. Now, they had started to watch these films with the children, and Astrid and Lars had filmed the children watching the film. As Astrid explained: 'Today, I have brought Axel's film, which also includes music. The children in the preschool liked this film very much because it has music. I have a movie of about five minutes, where we watch Axel's film'.

Sigrid explained that as project carrier, Astrid had chosen a number of themes that she wanted us to focus on: *the aesthetics, the language and communication*, and *the role of the pedagogue*. Astrid added that those who were in charge of language and communication could also watch for non-verbal communication. We were divided into groups of two, covering one of the three themes. My group comprised two pedagogues and me, in my role as researcher. Astrid explained that they had projected the children's films on the wall and had watched two films each time, but because the children had shown a particular interest in Axel's film because of the music, they had shown it a second time. Astrid turned on the film, and we watched the children dance in front of a big screen where we could watch Axel dancing.

After we had watched the film, Astrid urged us to take notes for some 2 or 3 minutes on what we had seen in relation to our theme and then talk about it in our group. I followed Sigrid and Selma, whose theme was the role of the pedagogue, to another room. Sigrid began by saying that she thought Lars was a bit passive. She thought it might have been better if the pedagogue was more present. She read from the *analytical schedule* provided, in which one of the columns included the Curriculum. The Curriculum said the preschool teachers should work as role models and stimulate and guide the children (Preschool Curriculum 2011: 4, 7). Sigrid wondered how it would have been if the pedagogue had danced along? She continued:

> The children move very freely, and there is nothing wrong with that. One child says: 'Axel dancing' and points to the screen, and the pedagogue confirms, but doesn't do more. And then in the end, a young child walks towards another child and wants him to dance. Then I think the pedagogue could have confirmed it and said something like 'you want him to dance with you'. (The term 'confirm' refers to wording, repeating, or reinforcing a statement so that the child feels understood.)

Selma thought it could have been a good idea to hide the computer, because there were a group of children focusing on the computer rather than the screen.

We moved back to the group, and Sigrid asked if they could start with *the role of the pedagogue*. Everyone agreed, and Sigrid asked Selma to summarize what they had said in her group. Selma said that one of them was filming, and the other pedagogue, Lars, sat among the children. Could he have engaged more with the children? Would it have been different if Lars had danced himself? Sigrid confirmed this point and added that she thought about the Curriculum and interaction with adults. Would it be possible to put the camera on a tripod, and be more involved with the children? She continued:

> And then I wondered. There were some children who were pointing out that it was Axel, and you confirmed that. And I think that is very good. But there was a child who was trying to get another child to dance. Sometimes you need to confirm the child, so that the other child understands what she means. Okay! That is what we had. Next group is *aesthetics*.

Sune started by saying that he noticed how the children moved, how they swung their bodies, how they imitated Axel. 'And they also stood in front of the projector, creating shadows. And one of them sat down and kept the beat. What did you see, Jonas?' Jonas said that he also saw the rhythm and how the children saw the shadows, and that they seemed to focus on how the shadows were playing on the wall. Jonas continued:

> They were also curious about the loudspeakers and the vibration they made. That might be something to explore further. It can be fun to put plastic film over the loudspeakers and then mix potato flour and water and put it on the plastic film to see how the vibration turns it into solid shapes.

Sune enthusiastically jumped in, saying that it is good to explore how they could improve. He continued:

> I saw fine motor skills and gross motor skills and body image. I see that as somatic learning. And how they reflect each other. It also shows proximal learning. And you could see that it created meaning for the children. I see, as in the Reggio-Emilia thinking, that we can learn in many different ways.

## 54  Meetings

Sigrid asked if they had more they wanted to say before she turned to the next group. Sune and Jonas shook their heads. Sigrid turned the floor over to Filip.

Filip started by saying that their theme was *language and communication*; the children didn't say much, so they had looked at how they moved and how they learnt from each other and from the film.

> We also talked about the girl who stretched out her hand, and we think she was able to communicate her message. You can see that they dance together later on. I'm thinking that the pedagogue was not needed, because they understood each other.

Filip was referring to Sigrid's comment that pedagogues could have confirmed. Sigrid urged Helen, the other member of the group, to contribute. Helen said absentmindedly: 'What did I say?' Then she focused and said:

> Some of the children know what dancing means. They have experienced dancing. But they have different ideas of what to do when dancing. One of the girls is running back and forth. But I also thought of the girl in the back who is observing. She is also part of the group, dancing a little bit. Some children want to be in the background.

Sigrid turned to the pedagogist,[1] Lovisa, who was responsible for pedagogical development in the preschool and part of the language and communication group, to give her the final say. Lovisa said that Filip had already mentioned much of what she wanted to say, but she wanted to say it somewhat differently.

> To focus on communication in such a non-verbal group is very interesting, because all the children are included and communicate in the film. Some of them stand around the computer with Lars, some of them stand in the back and observe. All of them are active. There is, in fact, a lot of communication in the room. I'm thinking about this idea of the *active agent*. How the material activates the children. You know this with objects and the environment, as active agents that we have been talking about, but that I have had a hard time wrapping my head around.

Sigrid confirmed that Lovisa had finished, then turned to Astrid for her to comment on the comments.

Astrid explained that they had had two different roles: She was documenting and Lars was with the children. She continued:

---

1 The concept of pedagogist [*pedagogista* in Italian – and in Swedish] is from the Reggio-Emilia pedagogy.

But to have a tripod is very good idea. I will bring that with me. We have photographed both around the computer and when they dance, but it's technically difficult in a photograph to capture children dancing. If you have any ideas of how to do it, I will be happy to receive them. The fact that we didn't help Milla when she was trying to get Nils to dance was because it was something I didn't see at the time. I had my focus on Edvin. It's interesting when you film, because you can see things afterwards. And Sune and Jonas. You didn't have any questions, but suggestions. We have also seen that the children explore many different things. They explore the light, the shadows, and the sound. It was a very good idea to use plastic film and potato flour.

Sune interrupted: 'I just remembered a question. As Sigrid said, if you would have been dancing with the children, what would had happened then?' Astrid answered:

Yes, when you said it, I immediately thought: 'Why didn't we dance with the children?' We will, of course, do that. And then we had Helen's, Filip's, and Lovisa's group. Yes, it's cool – the fact that they communicate in their own way. Milla managed to invite Nils to dance, as Fredrik said.

Sigrid reminded us that time was running out fast: 'Let's go around the table to see what everyone would bring with them'. Sune started by saying that he would bring back to the preschool the use of film, to see what happened regarding the three themes of the aesthetic, the language and communication, and the role of the pedagogue. Selma would bring back the idea that all the children participated in their own way, and that she could use a tripod. Jonas thought it was interesting that one could use the film to go back and see what happened, and that they could do more experiments. Helen considered it a smart idea to make a short film as a summer assignment with the small children, and Filip and Sigrid agreed. Astrid ended by saying that she had learnt a great deal, particularly with regard to non-verbal communication. Sigrid ended the meeting, and the pedagogues returned to their divisions and the children.

The architecture of pedagogical reflection meetings is not the same as the architecture of circle time or Lean board meetings. The pedagogues sit in the staff room wherever it is possible to see the project carrier, and when it is time for group discussion, they break into groups of two around the room before returning to the meeting. The focus here was on the pedagogical documentation presented by the pedagogue who brought the project. It was in the pedagogical reflection meetings that the pedagogical documentation and policy words from the Curriculum and the analytical schedule were practiced and circulated. Other practices circulating in the room were dialogue, reflection, and learning how to become better pedagogues. In this way, these meetings were also about improvement, but it was not improvement that focused on efficiency, but improvement that had to do with becoming better pedagogues and helping others to become better pedagogues. In this type of environment, how can Lean board meetings that focus on continuous improvement of efficiency and eliminating waste contribute to preschool activities? This was a question that the management of Birch Preschool Unit was trying to answer, and their solution was to try to make the preschool's information board into a Lean board to be able to have Lean board meetings, rendering Lean some of the preschool's planning and organization.

## Turning an information board into a Lean board

The Preschool information board (a whiteboard) was a critical instrument for the organizing and planning of preschool activities. It was usually placed somewhere to which all divisions in the preschool had access. In Bumblebee Preschool, it was placed in the staff room. Table 3.1 shows the information board in Bumblebee Preschool. (The names have been anonymized.)

Around the board were various policy documents on which the preschool was run. Three of these documents outlined the activities that took place annually. The *Pedagogical year* listed all the monthly pedagogical activities. The *Parental collaboration year* described all the monthly activities with parents and pedagogues, which were designed to fulfil the policy goal of having a welcoming preschool. And the *Organizational year* was outlined from the management group's perspective, and listed all its monthly planning and activities.

To explain how the preschool information board worked in daily practice, I must explain the preschool organization. Birch Preschool Unit consisted of four preschools: Bumblebee, Spider, Grasshopper, and Cricket, with a full-time employee Unit Head Christina and a pedagogist – Lovisa – responsible for pedagogical development. The management group, which met weekly, consisted of the unit head, Pedagogist Lovisa, and the four preschool heads – one for each preschool. The preschool heads were in charge of the daily activities in their preschool. The unit head worked as a full-time manager, whereas the preschool heads were first and foremost preschool teachers whose roles included management duties. In the management group meetings, the preschool heads were informed about activities that needed to be dealt with, such as writing the operational plan for their preschool in relation to the policies prioritized in the municipality politics or working with prioritized areas of improvement in the preschool identified by the annual user-satisfaction survey completed by parents on behalf of their children. It also included the work involved in pedagogical activities and the pedagogical documentation of the children, which had to be summarized and presented annually – first for the management group and then for the municipality.

Preschool Head Sigrid brought this information to the weekly meetings with the heads of each of the four divisions in the preschool. These meetings, which were held for one hour on Monday mornings, started with the division

Table 3.1 A copy of Bumblebee Preschool information board in one of the preschools translated into English

|  | Monday | Tuesday | Wednesday | Thursday | Friday |
|---|---|---|---|---|---|
| Division 1<br>Lina<br>Anette<br>Johan<br>Susann |  |  |  |  |  |
| Division 2<br>Hilda<br>Ingrid<br>Richard<br>Olga<br>Louise |  |  |  |  |  |
| Division 3<br>Rosanna<br>Ulrika |  |  |  |  |  |
| Division 4<br>Sigrid<br>Rosa<br>Nora<br>Laura |  |  |  |  |  |
| Lean | Bring up at the weekly meeting | Management group | Info | Deadlines | Courses | Order supplies |
|  | APT (workplace meetings)[1] |  | Areas of responsibility |  | To fix |

[1] *Arbetsplatsträff* in Swedish, also known as *APT* can be translated into 'workplace meetings', but they are more than workplace meetings. They are the result of collective agreements between unions and the employers and the so-called co-operation agreement that staff members need to be informed and heard in dialogue on the important issues of the organization – preferably once a month.

heads filling in the Bumblebee Preschool information board with such details as who was off sick in the division, who had to take time to order supplies from the supplier of diapers or crayons, or who had to attend a meeting – on fire safety, for example. Preschool Head Sigrid also noted deadlines for the operational plan or other organizational matters in the pipeline and informed the heads about what was happening. The preschool information board might also include the date that the children's photographs would be taken or a reminder to change the code on the entrance door of the preschool each year. Apart from planning and organizing the week, the weekly meetings of the heads also concerned issues that were particular for their preschool, such as the issues that they should bring up at the *APT* (workplace) meeting for the whole preschool, if they needed to change some routines, if they planned some reorganizing of the schoolyard, or how to involve parents in the parental meeting – issues that involved the whole preschool.

The rest of the week, each of the four divisions in the preschool had its own planning meeting for one hour every morning, while the other pedagogues took care of all the children in the schoolyard, including the children whose teachers were having a meeting. In these planning meetings, the week was planned in detail, including such issues as which of the children would present their project during circle time or where they would go for an excursion that week. They sat with their division paper calendar, filling in the pedagogical activities they were to offer and the organizational issues that needed to be dealt with during the coming week. Some of this also needed to be communicated in the weekly information letter to parents, especially if an excursion was planned, so that parents could ensure that the children were dressed suitably. Apart from the pedagogical issues, the division heads informed the teachers about issues from the management group and the weekly meeting of the division heads by going over the preschool information board and discussing what was happening. The teachers also informed the others about possible meetings they needed to attend, such as the pedagogical reflection meeting. If teachers were off sick in the division, attendances to some of these meetings might have to be cancelled. But the meetings were generally encouraged; attendance at the pedagogical reflection meetings, for example, was considered a significant part of the work of a preschool teacher.

The preschool information board and the weekly meetings of the division heads were significant devices for informing all the teachers in the preschool about what was happening that week and what was in the pipeline for the weeks to come. Unit Head Christina had the idea, however, that the weekly meetings could be changed into Lean board meetings involving the entire staff. Elm Preschool Unit, where I also worked, attempted to replace some weekly preschool meetings with a Lean-style meeting, with varying degrees of success (Thedvall 2015).

In the next chapter, I present the architecture and the practices circulating in Lean board meetings in Butterfly Preschool (part of Elm Preschool

Unit); suffice to say here that Lean board meetings should be short – meaning efficient – stand-up meetings, according to the model. Lean board meetings should also include the entire staff. As Unit Head Christina told me in an interview:

> Now we are working with representation at the weekly preschool meetings. And it is one thing to get second-hand information, and a completely different thing to get first-hand information. But in order to invite them all, we would need to have quicker meetings.

The need for quicker meetings was not only because of the Lean recipe for effective meetings, but also because someone had to take care of the children. Unit Head Christina envisioned that having a Lean improvement board meeting would result in the entire staff feeling greater responsibility for the work and organization of the preschool.

As a way of realizing Lean board meetings, Unit Head Christina, together with the municipality's Lean development strategist, Gunnel, invited the management group to take part in a Lean improvement-group meeting to figure out how they could use a Lean board and Lean board meetings rather than weekly meetings with a preschool information board. It was the spring of 2012 and I took part in this management group meeting in Birch Preschool Unit. Gunnel, the development strategist, distributed PowerPoint pictures of what a Lean board could look like. Christina started the meeting by saying that the point of this meeting was to create a preschool with a common identity, and she outlined some of the ways that she thought Lean could help them in that endeavour. She believed it could be done by working with so-called areas of responsibility. She continued by saying that they could, for example, use the Lean tool of 5Ss (sort, set in order, shine, standardize, and sustain the practice) within these areas of responsibility. She ended by saying that for this to happen, everyone had to assume greater responsibility. Gunnel took over. She was looking at the preschool information board and said:

> You start with what you have. You have most of the parts in the general improvement board, and then we need to connect it to a performance management board in relation to what Christina said about areas of responsibility. What you have here is an overview of the work activities, information from management. You also have what is in the pipeline about deadlines. You could add a column to write 'who is responsible' for the areas that Christina suggested. You also have information about the *APT*, the management group meetings, and the collaboration meetings. Performance management is related to the continuous improvement part. That's something you do every week or every day. What do you want to control against? It's possible to pick goals from the operational plan?

Gunnel was talking about the two Lean boards: the improvement board and the performance management board. The improvement board had various columns that provided such information as what needed to be improved and how it should be done. The improvement board was a way of visualizing who was responsible for what, and the point in the process they had reached in making an improvement. The performance management board included goals that could be evaluated and controlled. The board that they were looking at in the management meeting was the preschool information board that already existed in the preschool. Gunnel wanted the preschool heads to turn the preschool information board into a Lean board that had continuous improvement and/or performance management rather than information at the centre. She wanted them to choose goals that could be measured and enter them on the board to ensure that performance at the preschool was focused on these goals. She asked the preschool heads if they had some goals in the operational plan, which was the policy plan that had been worked out, based on the priorities in the municipality's budget for preschools. There were usually some political priorities included in the budget that needed to be handled by – in this case – the municipality's preschools. Gunnel continued by saying that if they picked three or so goals and entered them on the performance board, they could measure across a month; if they had a goal of 85 per cent and had reached only 70 per cent, they would know that they had a deviation. 'If you don't reach the goal, then you have a deviation. That is something that can be moved to the improvement board'. Gunnel continued by saying that it was important to make someone responsible for the improvement: 'It is also important to see your name on the board', she said. Pedagogist Lovisa interjected: 'There is a point in visualizing those who are responsible. It's good to see your name'.

Gunnel wanted the preschool heads to think about the board as a leadership tool. She wanted them to use the board to steer the staff towards continuous improvement and performance in focus. The Lean boards should then be used in Lean board meetings including all staff – not merely in the weekly meetings with the heads, who then informed the other teachers in their weekly planning meetings. Unit Head Christina suggested that they should divide into four groups for 15-minute sessions, ensuring that all employees took part in the Lean board meeting. The preschool heads were not convinced that this was a good solution. In fact, they vigorously protested, arguing that it would mean that they would have to give the same information four times, which would take an hour. It would also mean that some of the issues that they usually talked about in the weekly planning meetings would not be possible to discuss, and they wondered where they would discuss them. This entire conversation is recorded in Thedvall (2017), but suffice to say that the final solution from Gunnel was to have both the Lean board meetings and the weekly meetings, which meant that the idea of saving time was completely lost.

The preschool teachers needed an information board and meetings for the assurance that there was staff in all units or the assurance that everyone was informed about what everyone else was doing, so they did not book an excursion when some of their colleagues were having a meeting about Lean. Though Gunnel and Christina wanted them to focus on a Lean improvement board and a Lean performance board, substituting the weekly meetings with quick Lean board meetings did not make sense to the preschool heads. They needed the weekly meetings, which meant that they ended up with another meeting – the Lean board meeting. In the end, this preschool did not add another meeting, but attempted to modify its preschool information board to make it more readable according to the needs of staff members rather than those of the Lean model. (This issue is discussed further in Chapter 6.) The other preschool where I did fieldwork – Ladybug Preschool in Elm Preschool Unit – did implement a Lean improvement board and had Lean board meetings. I discuss them in greater detail in the next chapter.

## Conclusion: in the name of improvement

The focus of this chapter was on meetings as practices of performing policy. The meeting as a space has its own logic and constraints, making certain things possible while closing other doors. Policy is performed not only by the content of a meeting, but also through the way the meeting is organized. The practices circulating in meetings are limited by what the meeting as an event makes possible. The meeting as an architectural construct has its own aesthetics; the Lean board meeting sets the board at the centre, whereas circle time places the children at the centre. This may seem obvious, but it has an effect on the practices circulated in the meeting. Making the Lean board the centre means that improvement and efficiency are clearly in focus. Having children at the centre sets the focus on the way they co-operate, what they do together as a group. The pedagogical reflection meetings put the pedagogical project at the centre, where the architecture is built around the PowerPoint presentation and how the project can be improved, and ensures that it follows the Curriculum and the Reggio-Emilia pedagogy.

Meetings work as an event-that-models (Handelman 1990 [1998]), both as a model for the future and in the present, but in different ways. The Lean board meetings model for the future by focusing on improvement and efficiency, by working with the present through the board, focusing on such issues as evaluation, time lines, and employees listed as responsible for eliminating waste. The pedagogical reflection meetings also model for the future by focusing on pedagogical improvement. They are performed in the present through the use of a project and an analytical schedule focused on the Curriculum and the Reggio-Emilia pedagogy. Circle time, on the other hand, is based in the present and centred on taking attendance and by using dolls, songs, and voting, but circle time also works as a model for the future, in the sense that the goal is to make good, democratic, co-operating citizens who are prepared for school and work.

In this way, meetings make certain policy subjects, such as improvement-oriented employees or democratic citizens and project atmospheres, creating a policy environment that places particular issues at the centre, while others are prevented. Through its architecture, its organization, and its material artefacts, then, the meeting concentrates not only on a particular issue, but serves as a force, turning the meeting into a package with the power to change direction.

## References

Bailey, Frederick George (1965), 'Decisions by consensus in councils and committees', in Michael Banton (ed.), *Political systems and the distribution of power* (London: Routledge).

Basford, Jo and Wood, Elizabeth (2018), 'Assessment in early childhood education in England: Two readings, many lenses', in Jaipaul L. Roopnarine, et al. (eds.), *Handbook of international perspectives on early childhood education* (New York: Routledge).

Ben-Ari, Eyal (1997 [2013]), *Body projects in Japanese childcare: Culture, organization and emotions in a preschool* (London: Routledge).

Boden, Deirdre (1994), *The business of talk: Organizations in action* (Cambridge: Polity Press).

Brenneis, Donald (1994), 'Discourse and discipline at the National Research Council: A bureaucratic Bildungsroman', *Cultural Anthropology*, 9 (1), 23–36.

——— (2009), 'Anthropology in and of the academy: Globalization, assessment and our field's future', *Social Anthropology*, 17 (3), 261–275.

Brenneis, Donald and Myers, Fred (eds.) (1984), *Dangerous words: Language and politics in the Pacific* (Prospect Heights: Waveland Press).

Deming, W. Edwards (1986), *Out of the crisis: Quality, productivity, and competitive position* (Cambridge, MA: Massachusetts Institute of Technology, Center for Advanced Engineering Study).

Department of Education England (2017), *Statutory framework for the early years foundation stage: Setting the standards for learning, development and care for children from birth to five [England]* (United Kingdom: Crown copyright).

Goffman, Erving (1959), *The presentation of self in everyday life* (Anchor books; New York: Doubleday).

——— (1963 [1966]), *Behavior in public places: Notes on the social organization of gatherings* (New York: Free Press).

Handelman, Don (1990 [1998]), *Models and mirrors: Towards an anthropology of public events* (Oxford, UK: Berghahn Books).

Larkin, Brian (2013), 'The politics and poetics of infrastructure', *Annual Review of Anthropology*, 42 (1), 327–343.

Latour, Bruno (1986), 'Visualisation and cognition: Drawing things together', in Henrika Kuklick and Elizabeth Long (eds.), *Knowledge and society: Studies in the sociology of culture past and present* (6; Greenwich, CT: JAI Press).

Lillvist, Anne and Sandberg, Anette (2018), 'Early childhood education in Sweden: Policies, curriculum, quality and future challenges', in Jaipaul L. Roopnarine, et al. (eds.), *Handbook of international perspectives on early childhood education* (New York: Routledge).

Myers, Fred R. (1986), 'Reflections on a meeting: Structure, language, and the polity in a small-scale society', *American Ethnologist*, 13 (3), 430–447.

Olwig, Karen Fog (2011), 'Children's sociality: The civilizing project in the Danish Kindergarten', *Social Analysis*, 55 (2), 121–141.

Preschool Curriculum (2011), 'Curriculum for the Preschool Lpfö 98 revised 2010', in Skolverket (Swedish National Agency for Education) (ed.) (Stockholm).

Richards, Audrey and Kuper, Adam (eds.) (1971), *Councils in action* (Cambridge papers in social anthropology; Cambridge: Cambridge University Press).

Sandler, Jen and Thedvall, Renita (eds.) (2017), *Meeting ethnography: Meetings as key technologies of contemporary governance, development, and resistance* (Routledge studies in anthropology series; New York: Routledge).

Schwartzman, Helen B. (1989), *The meeting: Gathering in organizations and communities* (New York: Springer).

Senge, Peter M. (1994 [2006]), *The fifth discipline: The art and practice of the learning organization* (London: Currency Doubleday).

Thedvall, Renita (2005), *The meeting format as a shaper of the decision-making process: The case of the EU Employment Committee* (Score working paper series, 2005:1: Score (Stockholms centrum för forskning om offentlig sektor)).

―――― (2006), *Eurocrats at work: Negotiating transparency in postnational employment policy* (Stockholm studies in social anthropology; 58; Stockholm: Department of Social Anthropology).

―――― (2008), 'Rituals of legitimation: Organizing accountability in EU employment policy', in Magnus Boström and Christina Garsten (eds.), *Organizing transnational accountability* (Cheltenham: Edward Elgar), 131.

―――― (2013), 'Punctuated entries: Doing fieldwork in policy meetings in the European Union', in Christina Garsten and Anette Nyqvist (eds.), *Organisational anthropology: Doing ethnography in and among complex organisations* (London: Pluto Press), 106–119.

―――― (2015), 'Managing preschool the Lean way: Evaluating work processes by numbers and colours', *Social Anthropology*, 23 (1), 42–52.

―――― (2017), 'Meeting to improve: Lean[ing] Swedish public Preschools', in Jen Sandler and Renita Thedvall (eds.), *Meeting ethnography: Meetings as key technologies of contemporary governance, development, and resistance* (Routledge studies in anthropology series; New York: Routledge), 143–157.

Tobin, Joseph, Hsueh, Yeh, and Karasawa, Mayumi (2009), *Preschool in three cultures revisited: China, Japan, and the United States* (Chicago: University of Chicago Press).

Vree, Wilbert van (1999), *Meetings, manners, and civilization: The development of modern meeting behaviour* (London: Leicester University Press).

Womack, James P., Jones, Daniel T., and Roos, Daniel (1990), *The machine that changed the world: How Lean production revolutionized the global car wars* (London: Simon & Schuster).

# Chapter 4

# Colour

## Colours at work in play and in management

It's the autumn of 2013, and we're in a weekly work meeting at the preschool. One of the preschool teachers, Ingrid, brings out her smartphone and shows us a picture of happy, sad, and neutral emoticon faces in different colours. Green amplifies the smiling face; red, the sad face; and yellow, the neutral face. Or as it turns out, the colours are more important than the smiling or non-smiling faces, which merely serve to intensify the Lean management model colours of green, yellow, and red. 'We may be able to use these', Ingrid says. 'I found them on the table in [Unit Head] Christina's office. We can use the faces to express how we feel – if we are happy or sad'. Preschool Head Karla interjects: 'It's not about how you feel. It's about how you have experienced the workweek'.

Ingrid had accidently stumbled across the Lean way of evaluating the workweek. Karla had already used the symbols in the management group meetings as a way of evaluating her workweek. It was part of the municipality's focus on staff members feeling 'joy at work'; the underlying assumption was that if staff members became more efficient, there would be more time for the users – the children. And if there were more time for the children, the service would automatically become more qualitative, and therefore result in more 'joy at work'. To ensure that this happened, staff members were to evaluate their workweek to determine if there were 'not so joyous' occasions that could be improved – according to the logic, become more efficient – thus more qualitative, and thus more joyful. Karla wanted to clarify that it wasn't about feelings. It was about ways of improving the organization continuously by evaluating the workweek. In the management group, they had talked about using the symbols as part of the weekly preschool meetings, but they had not yet begun – thus Ingrid's confusion.

The Lean colours of green, yellow, and red are visible throughout the Lean management model. Their meanings differ depending on where they appear in the model (more about this later in the chapter), but basically the colours are modelled on a traffic light, where green stands for 'go/good', yellow for 'warning/neutral', and red for 'stop/bad'.

This chapter investigates the use of colours in preschools and management models by focusing on the role of colour in organizational practice. As Beyes

(2017) and Beyes and De Cock (2017) noted, there is need for a chromatic of organizations to establish how colour provokes, conditions, disrupts, and alters organizational conduct, practice, and form (Beyes 2017). It is necessary, therefore, to pay attention to the multiple political forces that colours both reveal and produce as they form the commanding elements of apparently mundane work practices and the ability of colours to evoke emotions and prompt affective reactions. By turning attention to the agency of colour, I want to shed light on its operations and power in Swedish public preschools, and in so doing, to investigate the agentive powers of colours. How do Lean colours become a tool for organizing preschools, and what kind of organizational, emotional, and material processes do they set in motion? How do colours work as a medium to intervene and transform the way in which preschools are conducted? Colours matter in many aspects in the everyday activities of preschools, in play and pedagogy, in working with children to express themselves through colours. Lean's green, yellow, and red are essential for the Lean management model to push for improvements, monitoring, and evaluation. In this way, the colours work as a tool for 'fast policy', adding to the 'model power' (Peck and Theodore 2015) of management models in the preschool environment.

The outline of this chapter mirrors the fact that Lean is a model that must be bolted on to the preschool staff's workload in caring for and educating children. In this chapter and in this book, I highlight the difficulties that the staff must face as they try to fit Lean into their daily activities – in moving back and forth between the Lean model and the everyday life of the preschool, demonstrating the tensions between the dispositions of the model, the dispositions of preschool work, and the requirements of preschool work. In the first part of the chapter, I undertake a brief exploration into the vast research literature on colour. In the following section, I present the Lean colours and the way they are meant to put organizational practices to work. I then turn to colours in the everyday activities of preschools, in play and pedagogy, as a way of contrasting the world of the Lean model and the world of preschools and children. In the following section, I highlight some of the preschool teachers' attempts to use the Lean colours and the efforts involved in having the Lean colours used for their improvement, monitoring and evaluation. In the conclusion, I contend that Lean colours work as a political force, pushing towards transformations into regulation, standardization, and control, and moving away from creativity and children's development.

## Colours as transformative and provoking responses

The investigation of how colours are used in organizations as tools for organizing, to transform and intervene in organizational practices, is a relatively new area of research (Beyes and De Cock 2017; Beyes 2017). Philosophical and anthropological interest in colours has a long history, however: the history of their meanings, the way humans see and understand them, their impact, their transformative capacity, and their material qualities (e.g. Benjamin 2011; Goethe 1812 [1971]; McGuin 1991). Early anthropological studies on colours focused on the relationship between language and colour perception and cognition. The Sapir-Whorf hypothesis (Sapir and Irvine 2002), based on the work of Edward Sapir and Benjamin Lee Whorf, focuses on the way linguistic structures influence human perception and the cognition of native speakers of a language. According to the hypothesis, speakers of different languages live in different perceptual worlds, thereby emphasizing linguistic relativity. The strong version of the Sapir-Whorf hypothesis is that language determines thought and the weak version is that it influences categories of thought. Does language determine or influence how a subject sees the colours of the rainbow, for example?

The Sapir-Whorf hypothesis was later challenged by Berlin and Kay (1969), who studied the universal nature of human languages and cognition through experiments with colours. They demonstrated universality in basic colour terms among human languages. Their study has been challenged on the basis of both data and method (Saunders 2000), but research on colour categorizations in language and thought has thrived and developed into an academic field of colour science (Hardin and Maffi 1997; MacLaury et al. 2007). These researchers examine how we see colours and understand them as a brain-based experience or sensation. A relativist account would argue, instead, that seeing colours is a cultural achievement, a tacit skill acquired through practice (Saunders 2000, 2007). According to this view, colour is not a simple phenomenon, but a concentration of determinations (Saunders 2000: 93). Colours are relational and social by nature, in that they become unstable and even invisible if deprived of the company of other colours (Massumi 2002).

Colour symbolism is another major field within colour research. In the early writings of anthropologists, researchers in this area attempted to classify colours into different domains and find universal patterns in the symbolism of each colour (e.g. Richards 1956 [1988]; Turner 1967). Turner (1967) found several meanings in the white, red, and black of the Ndembu[1] ritual, clustered in such a way that red stood for blood and kinship, white for good and harmony, and black for evil and death. According to Turner, the symbolism in these colours were connected to the body. Red, white, and black appeared as significant symbols related to the body in Bemba[2] ritual as well (Richards 1956 [1988]). The fact that red, white, and black appeared in rituals with several groups of people around the world spurred the interest of academics to create colour classification based on universal colour symbolism.

Later studies of the symbolic meaning of colour have focused on the production of colour symbolism through historical and political contexts. In this

---

1 The Ndembu tribe Turner researched was located in today's Zambia.
2 The Bemba tribe Richards researched was located in today's Zambia.

way, colour is a social phenomenon; society creates colour, its meanings, definitions, codes, and values (Pastoureau 2008). Thus, colour embodies social processes (Young 2006). As Taussig (2009) notes, colour embeds and reveals complex political histories; it comes across as 'more a presence than a sign, more a force than a code' (p. 6). The force of colours in political histories is shown, for example, by the so-called colour revolutions (cf. Manning 2007): The Yellow Revolution in the Philippines, which led to the toppling of dictator President Ferdinand Marco in 1986, or Ukraine's Orange Revolution, which led to a re-vote of the suspected rigged election of 2004. Colours have a wide-ranging political history. In the 19th century, British art teachers began offering skin-colour charts and standardizing colour terminology, giving birth to 'Indian yellow', as used in British representations of brown skin on paintings (Bailkin 2005). Indigo became the colour of authority, as represented in police and military uniforms – until it was transformed into everyone's colour through denim jeans (Taussig 2008, 2009). Purple became the colour of queens in 19th-century Britain, to the point that non-royals were not allowed to wear purple (Blaszczyk 2012). These colour histories are intertwined in the colonial past, when colours were a rare and often expensive commodity of trade and exchange.

The political past has also played a part in constructing green as a cultural identity and a way of signalling Irishness in the tourist offices and branding of Ireland (Wulff 2012). Colours and commodification are intimately intertwined (Baudrillard 1968 [1996]). With the development of synthetic colours in the 20th century, colours began to be mass produced, leading to the realm of current commodities (Beyes 2017). The first General Motors' colour engineers of the 1920s were employed to meet and stimulate consumer demand for cars in different colours (Blaszczyk 2012). Colours also work as a brand to entice consumption; Pan American World Airways' use of a distinctive blue, which came to be called Pan Am blue, serves as a good example (Blaszczyk 2012). Indeed an entire field within consumer and market research focuses on colours and brands, and the power of colours is well known in the advertising industry. The use of colour in commodities has also led to the engineering of colour standards, with businesses in colour forecasting upcoming fashions and furnishings, and other types of colour management simplifying production and giving aura to commodities and dazzle to consumption (Beyes 2017; Blaszczyk 2012). Thus, colours serve in a dual capacity: to enchant and to corrupt (Beyes 2017).

The magical, enchanting spirit of colours – or colours as a 'polymorphous magical substance' as Taussig (2009) puts it – signals that colours are 'this quite other medium', that is, both the 'the act and art of *seeing*' (p. 47). Colours have a fluid and spiritual nature, dancing from one context to another (Benjamin 2011); they can be harnessed to ideas, things, and events, and can accomplish work that no other quality can (cf. Young 2006). Colours are a medium of transformation (Benjamin 2011). Colours can animate and connect otherwise disparate ideas, things, and events. They have the ability to transform and produce a variety of effects and provoke affective responses (Fehérváry 2013). They have a material quality, though it seems difficult to separate them from the idea, substance, or form from which they are entwined; there is an abstracted property to colour that makes them separate (Beyes 2017). In this way, colours have agency, and they communicate. They thereby affect ideas and have the ability to transform ideas, things, events, and social relations (Eaton 2012; Young 2006).

It is the transformative capacity of colours and their ability to provoke affective responses that is investigated here in relation to Lean and the organization of preschools. My focus is not on what colour *is*, but on what colour *does*.

## Putting Lean colours to work

The Lean colours tap into a convention modelled on the green, yellow, and red of traffic lights. In the early days of the traffic light, only red and green were represented, but as vehicles became faster and traffic denser, the need for a third, warning colour was needed. Although history tells us that the first traffic light was invented in Britain by a railway-signalling engineer by the name of J.P. Knight and installed in London in 1868, the inventor of the first three-coloured traffic light is unclear. It is sometimes attributed to Detroit police officer William Potts, in 1920; other versions of the story place the first three-coloured traffic lights in New York in 1918. The first to patent the three-coloured traffic light, however, was Garrett Morgan. The patent was granted in 1923 and the three-coloured traffic light was installed in Cleveland, Ohio. The US Railway Signal Association (RSA) likely inspired the use of yellow as warning when, in 1908, it introduced the three Corning-RSA colours that became the informal industry standard (Blaszczyk 2012). So there is an established way of understanding green, yellow, and red, as used in the Lean model to transform, monitor, and evaluate flow on the assembly line.

Lean's green (good), yellow (not good), and red (bad) had slightly different meanings whether used to monitor or evaluate. As a performance instrument in the automotive industry, the Lean colours were employed in evaluating target compliance. In the *just-in-time* production line of a Lean car company, targets were set for the number of cars to be produced in order to keep pace with customer demands. A Swedish automotive company used the colours to signal the extent to which the assembly line was following the standardized production rate (Garsten et al. 2006) through electronic display boards positioned around the factory. If the production rate was being maintained, the display board read 'Should be 19' in red and 'Is 19' in green. In another department, where production rates were not being maintained, the board read 'Should be 19' in red, and 'Is 18' in red (Garsten et al. 2006). At other factories using the three Lean colours, the screen signalled green as long as the number of cars to be produced that day was on target. If production was in danger of falling behind, the screen lit up yellow, signalling 'delay'. And if the target was failing, the screen was red. Yellow and red were supposed to trigger workers into action, to reduce the delay and ensure that the number of cars produced would be able to satisfy customer needs.

The Lean colours were also used to identify waste that was slowing down the process or to stop the process if a machine broke down on the assembly line: the so-called *andon* – the line-stop indication board (Ohno 1988). Then when the problem was rectified, the colour changed to green. When a problem was identified and adjustments had to be made, a worker changed the colour to yellow. Red indicated that a stop was needed on the production line until the problem was resolved. As mentioned in Chapter 2, this was what Ohno called *autonomation* – automation with a human touch or giving human intelligence to the machine (Ohno 1988). In the Toyota plant, autonomation meant that humans should supervise the machines so they could detect malfunctions early in the process and push the stop button to ensure that waste was minimized (Ohno 1988). This system was expanded to the manually operated parts of the production line, so workers could push the button when detecting abnormalities (Ohno 1988). Stopping the whole production line also made everyone aware of the problem, eliminating waste by preventing overproduction and the production of defective products (Ohno 1988).

The colours were then put on a Lean board and used to evaluate the need for improvement on some of the production lines during short stand-up meetings in front of the board – the type of Lean board meetings explained in Chapter 3 – often before every shift. If a need for improvement in the assembly line flow were understood, it was suggested that a group of employees do a so-called *value-stream mapping*. I describe value-stream mapping in detail in Chapter 5, but for now suffice to say that if a problem with flow efficiency occurred, employees used value-stream mapping to identify *flow units* and *cycle time* in the production processes, to detect and eliminate waste (Modig and Åhlström 2012). The outcome of value-stream mappings was often a need for further action, which would end up in *action plans* that were monitored and evaluated in an effort to determine that the action was being taken according to the action plan. The Lean colours appear in both value-stream mappings and monitoring documents.

Lean colours on the assembly line of the automobile factory were used to provoke affective responses and to alert workers that the number of cars was falling behind and that they should close the gap between the target and the reality. The colours intervened in the organizational practice and set emotional and material processes in motion in the factory as the workers aimed for a green board, for having machines that function, and for having green flows on the *andon* board.

## Colours as play and pedagogy in preschool

Colours play a different role in preschools, not being intimately connected to evaluation, but to aesthetic qualities in the sensibilities of art teachers, pedagogues, and children. Colours play a significant role in the pedagogy of the Reggio-Emilia-inspired preschools. Reggio Emilia emphasizes the need for an atelier in the preschool, and it considers the children as having the ability to express themselves through *a hundred languages*, of which colours are but one (Wurm 2005). The importance of colours in preschools became particularly obvious when I was participating in a two-day planning activity in the autumn of 2013 in Bumblebee Preschool. By then I had spent several weeks in the preschool participating in painting and drawing activities in the atelier. It was fascinating to see how the 2- to 3-year-olds knew exactly what to do, even though not all of them strictly followed the protocol. They knew where to find the block of paints; they knew that they needed water and a brush; and they knew they needed a pinafore to protect their clothes, even if they needed help to put it on.

Charlie and Sarah were each standing in front of an easel. They wanted to paint, had donned their pinafores, had decided which colours to use, and had placed their colour blocks on a colour tray and filled their glass with water and brushes. Three easels were mounted on the wall at the appropriate height for 2- to 3-year-old children. Louise, one of the preschool teachers, had helped Charlie and Sarah to tape a paper on the easel. Now, they were in full swing, using their brushes to paint. Charlie was using green, yellow, and white paints, and although it was not obvious, he said that he was painting an elephant; a mixture of the three colours was appearing on the paper. Sarah was painting with green, red, and blue, what looked like a bug, but was supposed to be a bus. The aesthetic qualities of colour in the eyes of the children did not mean that colours necessarily had to match the conventional colours of an elephant or a city bus.

When Charlie and Sarah had finished painting, they had to clean their brushes. They seem to have as much fun standing against the sink cleaning brushes with water as they did painting. Using clothespins, Louise hung the paintings to dry on a string that was hung across the room. Some of the paintings ended up on the walls of the atelier and the other rooms in the preschool. They were usually connected to a pedagogical project, as when they painted with the help of Lego tyres in the project on buses or when they depicted animals by photographs of an animal. The walls were covered with the children's paintings from pedagogical projects. Charlie's and Sarah's paintings would be placed in their portfolios if Louise deemed them to be an example of the children's progress, or they would be put in the children's box for the parents to collect and decide what they wanted to save. In this way, there was an element of evaluation, but it was if the painting could show some progress in the child's learning. It was not, as in the English system, used to evaluate if the child reached the goals of the Statutory Framework for the Early Years (Department of Education England 2017) on a scale from 1 to 3, where the child needs to have at least a 2 to be understood as having reached a 'good level of development' (Basford and Wood 2018). Nor was it used to determine if the painting was good or bad (or in between) according to a Lean scale.

Colours and such other expressive tools as clay were grouped in the atelier, the biggest and one of the most important rooms in the preschool environment.

The Reggio-Emilia pedagogy also prescribed an *atelierista* – a teacher with background in the arts – as a central figure in the children's development. The atelierista helped the teacher and the children with colours and paints and other materials found in the atelier. The preschools where I was doing my fieldwork did not have an atelierista, but when I participated in the two-day planning activities, an atelierista taught a group of us about colours.

Atelierista Karin spent most of her time at the school teaching us about the material properties of colours and how to use them with children. She emphasized the need for children to work with colours and painting and especially encouraged us to paint and draw with the small children – the 1- to 2-year-olds – because she considered painting to be often neglected in that age group. She was teaching us about the colours to buy, establishing that we opted for colours that were rich in pigment, so the children would have high quality colours to work with, providing them with the enjoyable experience of sensing richness in the colours appearing on paper. She explained that they used to work with thick brushes for small children, but 'then they colour with only one colour, and it's not that developing. It's better to let them have thin brushes. Then they paint in a different way'. She showed us pictures of paintings by small children to emphasize her point that they did use different colours on the paper when they were supplied with small brushes.

She continued to advise us. Meanwhile we were asked to find the colours in the autumn leaves that had been placed on the table. We had to choose one leaf and try to mix the colours that matched the various colours and shades of the leaf. Karin continued to talk about the choice of the type of colours to have in the preschool and encouraged us to buy tempera blocks because tempera is cheap and better than plastic colours like acrylic. And she wanted us to have colour in blocks, which would allow the children to start by making a choice of colour blocks to put on their colour tray, thereby making it part of the pedagogy. She concluded by telling us about the colours we should have at the preschool. She said that we may think it would be the primary colours of blue, red, and yellow, but she wanted us to have the cyan, lemon yellow, blue with a tint of red, red, orange, brownish red, black, white, purple, ochre, and umber. By mixing these colours, the children could create a rainbow of colours to use on their paintings.

The conditions for colours differed completely between the preschools and the automobile factory – between children and cars. Colours in preschools were about teaching one of the hundred languages, to ensure that children could express themselves through colours by painting and drawing. Colours and painting was an affective and imaginative experience for the children, who could see an elephant among the brush strokes of green, yellow, and white. The pedagogical goal of children expressing themselves through colours was to teach them to speak the same colour language. It meant helping the children to find the 'right' colours of animals, by asking them to depict animals from photography, for example, but it was also to keep painting a joyful experience. So an elephant could definitely be green, yellow, and white.

## An aesthetics of evaluation

I went along with Lean Coach Mira to Butterfly Preschool in Elm Preschool Unit. The Lean coaches were administrators, social workers, homecare workers, workers caring for the elderly and disabled, and preschool teachers in the municipality – employees who had expressed an interest in being part of the municipality's investment in making itself a Lean organization. Like the others, who worked part-time as Lean coaches, Mira was a preschool teacher who worked in administration in Elm Preschool Unit and had asked to become a Lean coach. I was going to be participating in the first Lean board meeting at Butterfly. They used to have meetings with representatives from the different divisions within the preschool, but it had not worked well. Because information had been lost along the way, they opted instead for weekly Lean board meetings. The Lean board meeting was built on the idea that it should include everybody – just like in the automotive industry when factory workers gather in front of the Lean board before every shift. In order for it to work in preschools, they had to meet in shifts, because someone would have to take care of the children. Unlike cars, children cannot be left alone.

Lean Coach Mira divided the teachers into two groups. The teachers responsible for the younger children in Division 1 and 2 arrived at 9:00 a.m., and the teachers responsible for the older children in Division 3 arrived at 9:30 a.m. Thus two Lean boards – whiteboards in this case – were required. One of these whiteboards was already in place and divided into headings. The other hung empty on the wall. I helped Mira tape the columns onto the board with thin, black tape. One of the staff members, Silva, arrived early, ready to write the headings in the columns.

As explained in Chapter 3, Lean boards look different, depending on the needs of the workplace. They can be *improvement boards*, including headings demonstrating who would be responsible for the improvement, the time frame for the improvement, and its status or *performance management boards*, including the organization's objectives and evaluations of these objectives. The board being created at the preschool was an improvement board combined with a section on performance management. The improvement part of the board had the following headings:

*Förslag* (Suggestions)
*Vem* (Who)
*När* (When)
*Förbättringar* (Improvements)
*Ansvar* (Responsible)
*Klart* (Finished)
*PDCA* (Plan, Do, Check, Act – according to Deming's cycle (Liker 2004), indicating their position in the improvement process)
*Metod/Verktyg* (Method)

Table 4.1 A copy of Butterfly Preschool Lean board (a whiteboard) translated into English

| Suggestion | Who | | | | | When | | | Improvement | Responsible | Finished | PDCA | Method |
|---|---|---|---|---|---|---|---|---|---|---|---|---|---|
| | F | M | T | W | T | | | | | | | | |

| Name | Quick fix | | | Deviations | Area | Responsible | Finished |
|---|---|---|---|---|---|---|---|

At the bottom of the board was a performance management board, with another set of headings: Name, Friday, Monday, Tuesday, Wednesday, Thursday.[3] The performance board evaluated the municipal goal of *joy at work* as a way of detecting areas for improvement that could then be inserted on the improvement part of the board. Under *Name*, staff members wrote their names and evaluated each day with a green (good day), blue (normal day), or red (bad day) dot. The preschool used the blue to indicate that everything was fine, because it was considered more neutral than yellow, which tended to be seen as a warning – particularly paired with green and red, reminiscent of traffic lights. The change to blue speaks to the affective responses of colours.

The evaluation by colours pertained to the mood of staff members, and was performed by putting Lean colours of green, yellow, or red – preferably with smiling or non-smiling faces – on the Lean board. Lean Coach Mira had explained to me earlier that they had stopped using the green, yellow, and red dots with smiling or non-smiling faces. The same was true at another preschool, where the dots were changed to different shades of orange but the smiling and non-smiling faces were still used. In this preschool, green represented joy at work, blue or yellow meant *neutral*, and red stood for *not joyous at all*.

Staff members who put red beside their names on the board should ideally think of a way to fix the problem or think of a Lean tool that could be used to improve the situation. As Mira explained to the staff on the first morning of the Lean board meeting:

> It's important that you fill in the colour everyday so you don't forget. Otherwise it may be the same colour for each day if you forget to fill in what you actually felt that day. You put a green dot if you have a good example. When something has been especially good. Blue is if everything is fine. If it's moving along. If you put red, then you have to be prepared to explain what the problem is and give an example of how it can be better or how we can work to solve in together in the group.

The aesthetics of the Lean colours on the Lean board places evaluation at the centre. Lean is based on an ethics of evaluation (Thedvall 2015), whereby work processes need to be constantly evaluated to guarantee that targets are met and that *continuous improvements* are being made. It wasn't possible to translate the number of automobiles produced or the amount of waste on the production line into the situation in the Swedish preschools. There were some possibilities for translating the idea into hospitals, in which Lean had proved popular (see Chapter 2), as there is, in fact, a flow of patients. At a surgical centre in Saskatchewan, Canada, for example, they used green, yellow, and red to indicate

---

3 The order of the days was dependent on the fact that they had the meetings on Friday, to the Friday on the Board referred to the previous Friday.

'in flow', 'behind but will catch up', and 'way behind, need help'. They also used the colours to signal if they were up to speed on scheduling surgeries. Green stood for 'all patients done'; a green circle stood for 'waiting to fill surgery, but most is done'; yellow indicated 'almost filled – 10 per cent remains'; and red meant 'the week is not done yet'.[4]

In preschools, the Lean colours were used to measure the level of joy at work. Staff members who didn't feel joyous would use a red dot, and the group would have to think of an improvement to eliminate the problem so everyone could feel joy at work. Most preschool teachers were positive towards the board or at least did not question it. One teacher, Elisabeth, was a bit sceptical about what could be considered a *good example*. She thought it should be something about the organization of work – not merely something like a successful excursion. She was not sceptical towards evaluation by colours, however.

The Lean colours on the assembly line of the automobile factory were used to provoke affective responses that would trigger action, motivating workers to reduce the gap between the target and the number of cars falling behind. The Lean colours are therefore colours of transformation. They intervene in the organizational practice and set emotional and material processes in motion in the factory, as the workers aim for a green board and green on the *andon* board to indicate machines that function and production that flows.

Lean colours of the Lean board in preschools were used to trigger the idea of a green day, a feeling of joy at work. These were colours with a mission, in the service of the modern project, visualizing the mood of staff, but also an anticipated joyous, effective, green future without problems. The Lean performance board worked as a 'valuation device' (Hauge 2016), governed by an aesthetic of evaluation in which the colours played a key role, intervening emotionally into the organizational practices of preschools by targeting a joyous, green, preschool.

## A medium of transformation

When Lean Coach Mira and I arrived at Butterfly Preschool for the Lean board meeting, Preschool Head Melissa was already there. We would soon be having a board meeting with the two divisions at the preschool. Mira and Melissa remained standing, while I sat down to take notes on what was being said in the meeting. The teachers arrived and sat around the table. Melissa started the meeting by urging staff members to stand, informing them that that is the routine for Lean board meetings. One of the staff members responded: 'Is there a reason for us to stand up?' Melissa explained that it was so they would stay alert. Lean Coach Mira illustrated that point by slouching in a chair, noting that it

---

[4] www.youtube.com/watch?v=gY_DWO0Z7us accessed July 2018. 'OR Scheduling Daily Production Board Huddle – Surgical Assessment Centre' Saskatchewan Health Authority

is difficult to stay alert when slouching. As mentioned in Chapter 3, the Lean board meetings have a particular aesthetic: It was important to stand in front of the whiteboard. There was an underlying notion that meetings in which participants are seated have a tendency to drag on, because everyone is too comfortable, and it is easy to start talking about other things.

Melissa started the meeting by turning to the dots evaluating each day, starting with Friday. There was one red dot beside Anna's name. Melissa asked Anna to explain why she had put a red dot on the board, and Anna said:

> Yes, there have been many changes that I didn't know about. And there was the problem with staff members that didn't come to work in the morning. I don't know how we can find out if someone is sick. I don't want to have to call people. If one stays home, one has to call to make sure we know.

Lean Coach Mira, who was also a member of the administrative staff at the preschool, informed Anna that she should inform Preschool Head Melissa if a staff member is absent without calling to tell anyone. They should of course report. 'It is an obligation', she concluded.

Another teacher, Rebecka, demonstrated some of the absurdities that Lean can introduce by asking if she could raise another issue regarding this problem or if she should wait until the next meeting, given that she hadn't put 'red' on the board. Being pragmatic, however, Melissa invited her to bring it up now. Rebecka asked if they needed to call in or if it was enough to send a text message or e-mail? She finished by saying: 'I was unsure of what to do'. Melissa responded that they needed to call in, because the colleague they text may not be at the preschool either that day. Like Mira, Melissa seemed a bit surprised that such basic knowledge was not completely clear to the staff. Mira pointed to the board and said that they should put it on the board as a *Quick fix*: an improvement that does not require a group solution, but that the person introducing the problem is responsible for ascertaining its completion. Melissa continued with Monday, saying that there were some blue and some green dots.

Melissa asked: 'Why was it green?' Carolina answered: 'Well, I don't remember. But it was good day I suppose'. Melissa wanted Carolina to present a 'good example', in order to spread a positive atmosphere in the workplace and in order that staff members not choose green routinely without thinking about it. But Carolina wasn't able to explain herself. Melissa left Carolina and turned to Silva: 'And then we have Silva; you also had a green dot'. Silva responded that she had been at a Lean board meeting at Ladybug Preschool (part of the same preschool unit) and thought it was extremely interesting. She realized that they could do many things with the Lean board. She finished by saying that she would like to go to their meetings one more time to get more inspiration.

Melissa continued on to Tuesday on the board, where Alba had put two dots – one blue and one red – on the same day. Melissa said with a firm voice that they could only put one dot for each day. Another staff member asked: 'But if it is different before lunch and after lunch? What do you do then?' Melissa reiterated that there had to be only one dot per day, and Mira clarified the point by saying that they had to put the colour they felt when it was time to go home. Again, it points to the absurdities of evaluating and standardizing a day in one colour. Alba said that she had put a red dot because it was a sloppy closing of the preschool on Monday, so that when she came on Tuesday she had to start by trying to find the binder with the information needed when opening the preschool. And then she had to look for the portable telephones. She continued:

> I tried to find the telephone numbers for staff. It rained, and I decided to open the preschool indoors instead of in the schoolyard. But the staff went to the yard, and it became a mess. I thought perhaps we could decide to meet in the morning to decide what to do.

Mira said that it was quite obvious that they had to do that. Melissa concluded that they had to find a place to meet and plan how they would organize the day. Alba said that she also expected some curiosity among staff members to try to find out if someone was already in place and had organized and planned the morning. Mira urged them on by saying that they could meet in the hallway at 7:15 a.m. to go through the organization of the morning. She finished by saying: 'Write it on the board as a Quick fix'.

Alba continued by saying: 'And then we need a list of the staff telephone numbers. We need a telephone list. A list that's in the binder'. Melissa asked who would be responsible for putting together such a list. She wrote it on the board under the heading Quick fix. Alba responded that she could to it. Melissa put Alba's name on the board and asked her when it would be finished. Alba answered 'next Friday', and Melissa wrote it under the heading 'Finished'. Melissa also finished writing about staff members telephoning when out sick and wrote, while informing us that the entire staff was responsible for ensuring that this worked smoothly.

We then turned to Wednesday, which had several green dots. Carola said that even though she and Mika (another teacher) were there alone that day, everything had worked well. Melissa continued with rest of the week, then turned to the upper half of the board, where they had listed improvements to be made during the previous week's meeting. They had decided to do a Lean value-stream process for *arranging the day*, which meant that in the morning one staff member went through the list of who had called in sick and tried to ensure that there were enough staff members in all divisions of the preschool (also see Thedvall 2015). She asked rhetorically if they had decided on a day for the improvement group to meet and try to arrange the day according to Lean. 'When was it?' Mira answered that it would be in two weeks. One of the teachers, Doris, asked why it said 'Everyone' under the heading: 'Who'. Melissa answered that it was because everyone had mentioned it. Doris then asked why it said October 4, and Melissa answered that it was because it was first brought up on that date. Doris said that she hadn't been at those meetings, which was why she was wondering. Melissa responded: 'No, it's good that you ask. Here it says P, which means Plan, next step is Do'. Mira clarified that during the planning phase, anyone and everyone can give opinions, but when they turn to the Do phase, it is too late to voice opinions: 'Then we try what has been decided during the Planning phase'. What Mira was explaining was Deming's cycle of *Plan, Do, Check, Act* used on Lean boards to make visible the group's position in the process of improvement.

Alba raised her hand and said that she wanted to ask a question. She wondered about the Lean board meeting for Division 3. They would have their meeting after Division 1 and 2. Alba was referring to the fact that there were three divisions in the preschool. Divisions 1 and 2 (the divisions for the two younger children) had their Lean board meeting together and Division 3 had theirs after 1 and 2. If there were issues that were brought up on their Lean board meeting, Division 1 and 2 would not learn about it until next week when they had their next Lean board meeting: 'Doesn't it take a very long time? It will take a week before we know what they have suggested'. Melissa answered that if there were something urgent, they would have to inform them. Again the Lean board meetings highlighted how difficult it is to fit Lean into a preschool, where the staff needed to be divided into two groups, given that the model was based on the assumption that everyone could be present at the same time. Melissa concluded by saying that the Quick fixes they had suggested in this meeting would also be put on the board of Division 3. She then finished the meeting, and the staff left, while Melissa, Mira, and I waited for Division 3 staff members to arrive.

The use of green signalled joy at work, but it also enticed staff members to take action by urging them to provide a *good example*, thereby helping to create a positive atmosphere in the workplace. Blue, and particularly red, were colours of transformation, with the goal to return to or reach green. They intervened in the organizational practices and set in motion such processes as morning meetings in the hallway, composing a telephone list, and improving the process of *arranging the day*. In this way, the colours worked as a way of identifying problems in the name of continuous improvements, but only particular structural problems were identified, such as having a telephone list or phoning in when out sick. These may be easy problems to talk about in the group, but the Lean model and the board were also constructed in such a way that they encouraged finding waste in flow and structural processes rather than pedagogical and childcare problems. There is a movement in the exercise that points to a goal of turning the board green. There is a force in the colours fostering red improvement-oriented workers moving towards green.

## Visualizing the successes and failures of Lean

If the colours of the Lean management model signified management's attempt to motivate staff and promote certain activities, another feature of Lean colours is their use as tools for monitoring behaviour. If it were decided, through the evaluations by green, yellow (blue), and red that there was a need for an improvement group to find ways to improve – arranging the day, for example – then the result of these improvement-group meetings ended in action plan documents. The way the action plan documents were formatted and formulated anticipate the future filling of forms. The action plan documents prescribe action by including the need for follow-ups at 30, 60, and 90 days.

When the group of preschool teachers participating in an improvement-group meeting of the work routines in the morning were finished for the day, they had written seven action plans. It was the autumn of 2012, and Lean Coach Agnes asked them when they would be able to take action for each of the plans. One action plan was called 'making sure that arranging the day is solved by 8:00 a.m.'. Agnes asked if it would be ready by the 30-day follow-up on November 13 or by the 60-day follow-up on December 19. To arrange the day meant that one staff member went through the list of who had called in sick and tried to ensure that enough staff was available in all divisions of the preschool. Michael said that it shouldn't take long: 'We only need routines for moving the children and staff'. They agreed that arranging the day should be ready by November 13.

When November 13 arrived and the Lean coaches did a follow-up at the preschool, they hadn't yet been able find time to get the routines in order. They had a suggestion, but it had not been possible to have a meeting because too many teachers had been out sick. Lean Coach Agnes completed the form with yellow, meaning that it was initiated. The colours had a slightly different meaning in the monitoring document, but with the same idea of good, neutral, and bad: Green stood for *finished*, yellow for *initiated*, and red for *not initiated*. At the 60-day follow-up, they still hadn't been able to determine the routine. Preschool Head Michael informed us that it was much more difficult than he would have thought: 'It's difficult to prepare for all possible scenarios. It quickly becomes pretty complicated'. Lean Coach Julia asked them if they had continued to work with the routine. Michael said that he had worked on a new routine, but that he hadn't been able to discuss it with the others yet. Julia kept yellow in the *monitoring activities* document.

When we met again for the 90-day and final follow-up, Lean Coach Agnes reminded the group that at the 60-day follow-up, when they went through all seven action plans, some of the plans had turned yellow again, and that 'some we had put green were really more yellow'. Michael answered with a smile that it feels greener now. Agnes asked how the routine for arranging the day had worked out. Michael laughed and said they may have solved it, because they wanted to delete the action plan altogether. 'It's too complicated', he said. 'Now,

I call at around 7:45 a.m. and arrange the day, and it works. But it was a good idea'. Lean Coach Agnes didn't want to delete it, but said that Lean is about what is best now, and we can keep it yellow, and then try again in the future.

According to the action plan document, the Lean colours of the monitoring document were meant to force action, with the colours working as a medium of transformation to guarantee that the action moves from red to green, from not initiated to finished. The sole purpose of the colours of the monitoring documents is evaluation and holding people accountable, keeping the process of action going by having 30-day follow-up intervals. The colours intervene in the organizational practice by forcing the preschool teachers to put effort into structuring and standardizing – into arranging the day. It turned out that finding a system became too difficult, and they returned to their old system of arranging the day by having one person responsible (Thedvall 2015). Yet, the monitoring documents ensured that the process did not end, as demonstrated by Agnes's wish to keep it yellow, urging them to try again in the future.

## Conclusion: Lean colours as a political force

If the Lean colours come with a mission to transform, colours in preschools are used to educate and entice play. My aim in this chapter was to visualize the dispositional differences between the Lean model and preschool work practices and the difference between what the Lean model can accomplish and what preschools need. The Lean colours focused on improvements, monitoring, and evaluations, where green was the goal and yellow and red indicated that there was a need for processes of transformation. The goal for the Lean model was a green and joyous future with green functions and flows, and the fostering of red improvement-oriented workers moving towards green. There is a motion in Lean towards the perfect organization, with smooth-flowing routines and standards. The Lean colours play a part in realizing this endeavour. In preschools, the pedagogy consisted of teaching the children about colour as one of the hundred languages, to verify that they could express themselves through colours by painting and drawing, while keeping the process joyful and eventful. Colours and colouring in preschools should be an affective and imaginative experience, with colourfulness as the point of departure.

The Lean colours intervene in the organizational practices of preschools by representing an aesthetic of evaluation that is set to alter organizational conduct, practice, and form. The preschool teachers are in front of Lean boards to evaluate their day in colours, or they are forced to participate in monitoring exercises in relation to what they have promised to do in action plans. In this way, the colours represent a particular way of organizing work, and disrupt earlier practice and conditions. The colours have agentic power. They provoke affective responses by compelling the preschool teachers to understand green, yellow/blue, and red in relation to joy at work. The Lean colours require the preschool teachers to invest in structuring and standardizing organizational work processes that have little to do with pedagogy and childcare, and more to do with routines. Routines, which they already had in abundance, especially for preschool activities, became the preschools' focus, rather than solving problems in pedagogy and childcare.

In this way, Lean colours work as political force pushing towards transformations into regulation, standardization, and control, moving away from creativity and children's development. Lean colour schemes clearly do not map the same meanings that colour in preschools have. And even if we removed the colours and focused on the evaluation, the Lean board evaluations and the Lean monitoring documents move away from pedagogy and care into the search for waste in flows and structural problems.

## References

Bailkin, Jordana (2005), 'Indian yellow: Making and breaking the imperial palette', *Journal of Material Culture*, 10 (2), 197–214.

Basford, Jo and Wood, Elizabeth (2018), 'Assessment in early childhood education in England: Two readings, many lenses', in Jaipaul L. Roopnarine, et al. (eds.), *Handbook of international perspectives on early childhood education* (New York: Routledge).

Baudrillard, Jean (1968 [1996]), *The system of objects* (London: Verso Books).

Benjamin, Walter (2011), *Early writings (1910–1917)* (Cambridge, MA: Belknap Press of Harvard University Press).

Berlin, Brent and Kay, Paul (1969), *Basic color terms: Their universality and evolution* (Berkeley, CA: University of California Press).

Beyes, Timon (2017), 'Colour and organization studies', *Organization Studies*, 38 (10), 1467–1482.

Beyes, Timon and De Cock, Christian (2017), 'Adorno's grey, Taussig's blue: Colour, organization and critical affect', *Organization*, 24 (1), 59–78.

Blaszczyk, Regina Lee (2012), *The color revolution* (Cambridge, MA: MIT Press).

Department of Education England (2017), *Statutory framework for the early years foundation stage: Setting the standards for learning, development and care for children from birth to five [England]* (United Kingdom: Crown copyright).

Eaton, Natasha (2012), 'Nomadism of colour: Painting, technology and waste in the chromo-zones of colonial India c.1765–c.1860', *Journal of Material Culture*, 17 (1), 61–81.

Fehérváry, Krisztina (2013), *Politics in color and concrete: Socialist materialities and the middle class in Hungary* (Bloomington: Indiana University Press).

Garsten, Christina, Lindvert, Jessica, Jambrén, Niklas and Thedvall, Renita (2006), 'From employment to the development of workers' capabilities: Mobility, learning and responsibility in Swedish worklife' (Report for the European Commission).

Goethe, Johann Wolfgang von (1812 [1971]), *Goethe's colour theory*, Arranged and ed. Rupprecht Matthaei; English edition trans. and ed. Herb Aach (London: Studio Vista).

Hardin, Clyde L. and Maffi, Luisa (1997), *Color categories in thought and language* (Cambridge: Cambridge University Press).

Hauge, Amalie Martinus (2016), 'The organizational valuation of valuation devices: Putting Lean whiteboard management to work in a hospital department', *Valuation Studies*, 4 (2), 125–151.

Liker, Jeffrey K (2004), *The Toyota way: 14 management principles from the world's greatest manufacturer* (London: McGraw-Hill).

MacLaury, Robert E., Paramei, Galina V., and Dedrick, Don (2007), *Anthropology of color: Interdisciplinary multilevel modeling* (Amsterdam: John Benjamins Publishing Company).

Manning, Paul (2007), 'Rose-colored glasses? Color revolution and Cartoon Chaos in Post-socialist Georgia', *Cultural Anthropology*, 22 (2), 171–213.

Massumi, Brian (2002), *Parables for the virtual: Movement, affect, sensation* (Durham: Duke University Press).

McGuin, Marie (1991), 'Wittgenstein's "remarks on colour"', *Philosophy*, 26 (258), 435–453.

Modig, Niklas and Åhlström, Per (2012), *This is Lean: Resolving the efficiency paradox* (Stockholm: Rheologica Publishing).

Ohno, Taiichi (1988), *Toyota production system: Beyond large-scale production* (London: CRC Press).

Pastoureau, Michel (2008), *Black: The history of a color* (Princeton, NJ: Princeton University Press).

Peck, Jamie and Theodore, Nik (2015), *Fast policy: Experimental statecraft at the thresholds of neoliberalism* (Minneapolis: University of Minnesota Press).

Richards, Audrey (1956 [1988]), *Chisungu: A girl's initiation ceremony among the Bemba of Zambia* (London: Routledge).

Sapir, Edward and Irvine, Judith T. (2002), *The psychology of culture: A course of lectures* (Berlin: De Gruyter).

Saunders, Barbara (2000), 'Revisiting basic color terms', *Journal of the Royal Anthropological Institute*, 6 (1), 81–99.

——— (2007), 'Towards a new topology of color', in Robert E. MacLaury, Galina V. Paramei, and Don Dedrick (eds.), *Anthropology of colour: Interdisciplinary multilevel modeling* (Amsterdam: John Benjamins Publishing Company), 467.

Taussig, Michael (2008), 'Redeeming Indigo', *Theory, Culture & Society*, 25 (3), 1–15.

——— (2009), *What color is the sacred?* (Chicago: Chicago University Press).

Thedvall, Renita (2015), 'Managing preschool the Lean way: Evaluating work processes by numbers and colours', *Social Anthropology*, 23 (1), 42–52.

Turner, Victor (1967), *The forest of symbols: Aspects of Ndembu ritual* (Ithaca, NY: Cornell University Press).

Wulff, Helena (2012), 'Color and cultural identity in Ireland', in Marilyn DeLong and Barbara Martinson (eds.), *Color and design* (London: Berg), 101–109.

Wurm, Julianne (2005), *Working in the Reggio way: A beginner's guide for American teachers* (St. Paul, MN: Redleaf Press).

Young, Diana (2006), 'The colours of things', in Chris Tilley, et al. (eds.), *Handbook of material culture* (London: Sage Publications), 173–185.

Chapter 5

# Flow
Eliminating waste along the assembly line

---

We were sitting in groups of four in the Lean coach-training course. It was the autumn of 2012, and Lean Consultant Karin asked us to designate a person in the group to be responsible for the Post-its®. Our group decided that Marjorie, an administrator in the Social Services, would be responsible and I would be her co-worker. Mira, a preschool teacher, was selected to be our timekeeper and would give us 90 seconds for our task. Camilla, caregiver for the elderly, was the controller. Lean Consultant Karin gave us instructions. Marjorie was to draw a cross on ten Post-its at a time and give them to me. I was to draw a circle around the cross on ten Post-its at a time and give them to Camilla for inspection. In the first round, we were able to put crosses and circles on 20 Post-its. In the next round, Karin asked us to give the Post-it to the next person in a flow as soon as we had drawn the cross and the circle rather than passing them on in a bundle of ten. This time Marjorie, Camilla, and I were able to finish 39 Post-its.

In order to learn about Lean in general and how it was being taught within the municipality, I was participating in a three-day Lean coach-training course in the municipality where Preschool Units Birch and Elm were located. The Lean coaches were administrators, social workers, homecare workers, preschool teachers, and workers caring for the elderly and disabled in the municipality – employees who had expressed interest in the municipality's support of Lean organization. They became Lean coaches by participating in a Lean coach-training course like this one, and were then able to work part-time as Lean coaches in the municipality. The Lean coach-training course entailed three full days of lessons from two consultants and a day of shadowing established Lean coaches. I was involved as a participant-observer in the three-day training course and I did days of shadowing (albeit as a researcher), which meant that, just like the other participants, I am now a Lean coach.

It was during this training that we were taught about efficient flows and about the advantages of keeping the flow going smoothly and regularly. In the Lean model, this means paying attention to the circumstances that are *stealing time* in the work process, by identifying *flow units* and *cycle time*, to enable, detect, and *eliminate waste* through Lean *value-stream mappings*, for example (Modig and Åhlström 2012).

This chapter investigates flows in preschools and management models. It focuses on Lean's premise of efficient flows, the elimination of waste in the Lean management model, and how this is played out in preschools. The notion of efficient flows highlights what Rosa (2017) calls 'the escalatory logic of modernity' (p. 34), in that modernity requires systematic growth, innovation, and acceleration, making room for 'fast-policy' (Peck and Theodore 2015a). The promise that smooth flows and efficiency would eliminate waste provides Lean with 'model power' (Peck and Theodore 2015b). I argue that Lean is a socially produced smoothing machine (Bogard 2000), set to smooth flows by eradicating waste in production processes. This requires that attention be paid to what is understood as waste by the Lean smoothing machine. Lean has its own classificatory system of what is 'matter out of place' (Douglas 1966 [1991]), neatly produced in the model by determining Lean's waste. The main focus is the dynamic and performative role played by waste in making efficient flows in the Lean smoothing machine and how it relates to preschools. How is waste classified in the Lean model? What flows can be made more efficient? What can be considered a flow in need of efficiency in preschools? How is the Lean smoothing machine played out?

The outline of this chapter reflects the fact that Lean is a model that must be bolted on to the work processes of childcare and the education of children in preschools. In it I highlight the difficulties of fitting Lean into the daily activities of Swedish preschools by moving back and forth between the Lean model and the everyday life of the preschool, demonstrating the tensions between the dispositions of the model, the dispositions of preschool work, and what preschool work requires. In the first part of the chapter, I present a brief exploration into the research literature on smoothing machines, waste, and excess. In the following section, I present the 8 wastes that Lean proponents look for when performing Lean value-stream mappings, in order to increase flow efficiency. I then turn to possible flows in the everyday life of preschools, first by presenting a possible flow that could be made more efficient in line with the Lean model, in which children would be cars on the assembly line. Fortunately, this had not occurred to the teachers, who instead tried to invent flows in their organization. The final two sections in the chapter focus on such attempts. In the conclusion to this chapter, I contend that there is no smoothing machine that can align and smooth between Lean and preschool care and pedagogy.

## Smoothing machines and efficient flows

Inspired by Deleuze and Guattari's (1987) notions of smooth space and striated space, Bogard (2000) asks the reader to imagine society as a production of 'smoothing machines', highlighting our society's fascination for smoothness, for flows that are efficient and fast without friction. I argue that management models can be seen as socially produced 'smoothing machines' – models that continuously create and re-create machineries and tools to smooth and make flows efficient and smooth flowing, affirming the modern fascination for smoothness, for free flows, for clean and fast production – a society with perfect bodies, perfect children, perfect homes, perfect work, in which everything disappears if perceived as unnecessary disturbances to achieving our goals and desires. As Bogard contends, the location of smoothing machines is at the interface between tool and hand, between hand and idea, between percept and affect, between word and thing. Smoothing machines are surfacing machines (Bogard 2000). Where there is a cut, a marking, or an inscription, smoothing machines smooth and align. Smoothing machines cut and grind to cover, coat, and align. In this way, no smoothing can occur without a break, a separation. Smoothing and marking are always combined: 'To smooth is to blend – blend in, disappear' (Bogard 2000: 288). Lean works as a smoothing machine at many levels, fitting one unit to the other, working on the interface between ideas and tools, tools and working units, work units and work processes, making smooth-flowing assembly lines and co-coordinating movement in a straight line. The straight line as an icon of modernity works as a sign of progressive advancement (Ingold 2007 [2016]). It resonates with theories on mobility and movement, permeating modern society, as something progressive, exciting, and contemporary (Cresswell 2006; Salazar and Jayaram 2016).

As a smoothing machine, Lean is meant to increase value by contributing to efficient flows and eliminating waste. The eradicating of waste is a key to the Lean process. The notions of waste and excess have raised scholarly interest within the social sciences, not at least by Mary Douglas (1966 [1991]). Douglas makes us aware that when there is dirt there is a system. Douglas's study of pollution points to the uncertain and undetermined nature of waste, in that it is not a fixed category, but an effect of classifications. Waste is not a stable category – not even as waste. The ontological shifts of waste become especially visible in the recycling of waste (Woolgar and Neyland 2013). Waste has been central to theories of value (Frow 2003) and is often understood as that which is discarded or expelled, without value (Hawkins 2006). As Thompson (1979 [2017]) has noted, it is not possible to create value without creating non-value. And as Bauman (2001) has noted, in order for norms to exist, they require excess as their counter pole. Waste is central to the formation of value. There are constant value shifts and value transfers, and objects often have multiple regimes of value (cf. Thompson 1979 [2017]).

Waste is intimately connected to the modern household, where technologies of convenience are promoted as labour-saving devices to make it more efficient, generating waste through consumption (Hawkins 2006; Strasser 1999). Strasser (1999) chronicled waste from the days of thrift and habits of reuse, through the throwaway culture of modernity, to today's mainstreaming of recycling. She argues that reading history through trash reveals hidden parts of history. The paradox is that wastefulness and excess are expected in a commodity culture (Bauman 2001; Hawkins 2006); whether measured in goods or time, they constitute methods of signifying wealth (Veblen 1899 [1932]).

Mauss (1925 [2002]) described the potlatch as a competitive and deliberately excessive system of gift-giving, waste, and excess used to establish and enhance social status. In the efficient Lean factory, quite the opposite is true: Wasted time and wasted energy by unnecessary motion is under attack. In Taylorist fashion, all useless movements should be eliminated, in the interest of saving time (Taylor 1911 [2006]).

It is the classificatory systems of waste and the dynamic and performative role played by waste in the Lean smoothing machine that is explored here. The consequences for preschools of these ideas of efficient flows and Lean waste serve as the main focus of this chapter.

## The flow of Lean

One of the main Lean tools is value-stream mapping. If a problem were identified with flow efficiency, employees could use value-stream mapping to clarify what was stealing time on the assembly line by identifying flow units and cycle time in the production processes, to enable, detect, and eliminate waste (Modig and Åhlström 2012). If a lack of flow efficiency appears on the assembly line, it is put on the *improvement board*, and a group of employees is identified to solve this problem in the best possible way. The group then meets in an *improvement-group meeting* to undertake a value-stream mapping. As Lean guru Liker (2004) has argued, *value-added time* is only a small percentage of the total time. The goal of value-stream mapping, therefore, is to eradicate, as much as possible, the *non-value-added-time* identified as waste. The process of identifying waste should centre on what creates value for the perceived customer. There are processes that are wasteful and create no value but that are required for production in the short run, and there are actions that create no value for the perceived customer and can be eliminated immediately (Womack and Jones 1996). The waste that is required in the short run to keep production going should be eliminated long term, whereas waste that creates no value and is not necessary to keep the assembly line running should be eliminated immediately. The elimination of waste is part Ohno's system of flow management, now called *just-in-time*, which means that in the flow process 'the right parts needed in assembly reach the assembly line at the time they are needed and only in the amount needed' (Ohno 1988: 4).

The first step in a value-stream mapping is to map the *current state* by identifying each flow unit. It is important to identify each element or unit in the work process. A value-stream mapping in an automobile factory begins at the receiving dock, where each workstation is identified as a flow unit, all the way to the customer. The next step in the process is to map the *desired state*, and the gap between the current state and the desired state is identified as waste. The 5 *Whys* are used to help employees remember to continue asking 'Why?' at least five times, assuring that they arrive at the root of the problem. The Lean model also comes with identified wastes in the form of the *8 wastes* tool, to be used when going through the production line designed to search for (1) overproduction, (2) waiting, (3) unnecessary transport or conveyance, (4) over-processing or incorrect processing, (5) excess inventory, (6) unnecessary movement, (7) defects, and (8) unused employee creativity. When documenting the desired state and the waste that is identified as non-value-added time, the *A3* document (printed on A3 paper) could be used: Staff members write down the problem, the background to the problem, the current state of affairs, an analysis of the problem, the desired state, the plan, the implementation plan, the monitoring, and the decision. For the final four stages of the A3, staff members should use Deming's Cycle Plan of *Plan, Do, Check,* and *Act* to ensure that they follow through with the decision that was made in order to eliminate the waste. (Also see Chapter 6.)

Value-stream mapping should be performed on each line in the factory, but each flow unit, each station, should also be flow efficient, which requires its own value-stream mapping to detect waste. Instead of mapping the assembly line of the factory, each flow unit is mapped, resulting in a *standard work sheet* posted at each station (Ohno 1988). The work sheet includes cycle time – the time allocated to make one piece (Ohno 1988). It consists of the *work sequence*, which refers to the order of processes along which production flows (Ohno 1988). And it contains the *standard inventory*, which should be kept to a minimum – preferably only with items mounted on the machines, because the parts for production should arrive just-in-time.

Through the value-stream mapping of the lines and the flow units, the factory should work efficiently, with smooth flows and no waste. The classificatory system of Lean waste is based on the idea that movements that do not add value to the perceived customer must be eliminated. It is about saving time, compressing time, in order to attain efficiency. How would this translate into life in preschools?

## Assembling in the yard to move into the preschool

The notion of a flow on an assembly line, where there is cycle time and flow units, is not easily transported into preschool activities. When using the Lean tool, teachers had to invent a flow that could be made more efficient. How that played out is described in the following sections, but I first want to explain the setting – the preschool where, in strict Lean terms, children would be the cars on the assembly line. As Radnor et al. (2012) identified in the English National Health Services (NHS), the Lean notion of the *customer* and the Lean goal to add value to the customer and remove waste that does not add value is difficult in public services. Is the customer the patient, those who commission the service, or political representatives in government? What is the car and who is the customer? In the Radnor et al. study of the NHS, most medical doctors interviewed identified the patient as the customer. The added value to the customer – the patient – would then be that the patient flow is more efficient, ensuring that the patient receive care earlier than if the patient flow had not been Leaned. The patient is then both the car and the customer. If the child is both the car and the customer, then efficient flows do not add value. There is no 'child flow' in preschools. Or perhaps the parents and society are also customers, as the development strategist for the municipality explained to me. And the main assignment for preschools is to educate and care for the children for the parents and society. Yet, given that Lean focuses on the core activities and on adding value to the perceived customer, then children would still be cars in order for the Lean model to work.

There are, of course, movement and flows in preschools, and I'm sure the teachers would sometimes have liked the children to flow as smoothly as cars on an assembly line when moving from the preschool yard into the preschool. But these processes are also part of children's learning about standing and waiting in line in the yard, taking off their outerwear in the hallway, then returning to the preschool division to engage in play, circle time, or a pedagogical project.

I was with the group of 2- to 3-year-olds, and it was time to leave the yard to move inside. It was the autumn of 2013 and one of the teachers, Karla, asked the children to assemble in a line along the wall beside the door; another teacher, Ingrid, stood with them. Some of the children followed the instruction to the letter; others were leaving the line, doing other things and going against the teacher's instruction. When six children had been checked off the list of those present that day, Ingrid started to walk inside with the first group, and I went along with them. The hallway where they hung their outerwear was downstairs, so we had to start by waiting for the elevator to go down one flight of stairs. The children ran into the elevator, but they all knew that they were not allowed to press the button to go down. Ingrid explained to me that it was impossible to let the children push the button, because they often ended up in arguments and fights over who did it last time and whose turn it was. It was easier to decide that only the teachers could press the button. A time-saving rule they did not need Lean to detect and decide even though that could have been an outcome of a Lean value-stream mapping of the movement from the preschool yard into the preschool.

When we arrived in the hallway, the children started removing their outerwear more or less successfully. It was late autumn or early winter, and all of them had boots and one- or two-piece snowsuits. They walked around like cute little Michelin people.

The children first tried to remove their boots before entering the area where shoes were not allowed – helped by the bootjack specially designed for small children, with a handle that they could hold in order to keep their balance. Some of them managed and others needed help. All the children had their own space where they hung their clothes, with their photograph above the coat hooks, but they already knew which space was theirs. One of the children, Isabella, ignored the bootjack and sat down on the floor, efficiently removing her snowsuit and boots, all in one go. Because the boots were attached to the snowsuit by elastic bands, it became a neat package that she tried to hang on her coat hook, and after some time was able to accomplish that task as well. Some of the smaller children needed help removing their snowsuits, because they had trouble with the zippers.

When the children had removed their outerwear, they were encouraged to sit on the shelf below their coat hook that was intended for the boots to wait until everyone had finished undressing. Some of them did so patiently, while others didn't, and Ingrid and I had to remind them constantly. When everyone was finished, we moved up the stairs to the preschool area. The children who didn't wear diapers anymore were sent to the communal washroom with two small-size toilets in a row, while the children with diapers were being changed. Then they washed their hands before we entered the atelier and the other rooms in the preschool. Before we turned to project time, Ingrid marked on the pee and poo chart – small-size whiteboard with each child's name – who had done what, so that parents could read it when they picked up their children in the afternoon.

I'm sure the teachers sometimes felt that a smoother flowing process could be accomplished with children standing in line and efficiently removing their outerwear. At the same time, the teachers were experts in seeing every occasion as a learning occasion, patiently waiting for children who struggled to remove their boots or snowsuits or taking the time to explain why it's important that they do stand in line or wait for their friends. 'Friends' was always the term used, and used in the same way I would use the word 'colleague'. In Lean terms, however, this flow could be made more efficient, because that was the whole idea of Lean. Children who were not as efficient as Isabella in taking off their boots and snowsuits would be considered waste in the 'removing outerwear flow unit'. Fortunately, it never occurred to the teachers that children should be treated like cars on an assembly line that should flow as efficiently as possible. Rather, they tried to think in terms of the flows that could be Leaned.

## Learning how to complete a value-stream mapping

Now to return to the Lean coach-training course mentioned in the beginning of this chapter.

We were seated in groups of four as if we were in a Lean improvement-group meeting doing a value-stream mapping. Mira, one of the members of our four-person group, was a preschool teacher. She presented the recurrent problem of being unable to finish the pedagogical documentation in time, and our group decided to use that example when trying to learn how to do a value-stream mapping. As explained in Chapter 3, pedagogical documentation is a tool for organizing pedagogical work. To do pedagogical documentation, the teachers first observe and document the children around a specific theme – sand, water, or stones, for example – which had been decided upon beforehand. The idea of working with a theme is also part of the Reggio-Emilia-inspired preschool. The teachers show the documentation in the form of pictures and/or texts to the children during the assembly, and the children reflect and analyse. This *reflection* is also documented, and the teachers reflect upon, analyse, and interpret the original observation and the children's reflection in the *pedagogical reflection* meetings chronicled in Chapter 3. According to Reggio Emilia, nothing can be called pedagogical documentation until it has been reflected upon, analysed, and interpreted by both children and teachers (and, if possible, parents).

We were required in the Lean coach-training course to identify the problem and the goal, and how to measure if the Lean process had delivered results. Mira formulated the issue: 'The problem is that one begins the documentation, but one does not finish. It stops and then one has to start over'. Mira said that the goal must be to write clear pedagogical documentation. Marjorie added that it should be completed in one go, without interruption. Camilla wrote the document and read to the group that the goal is 'to write clear pedagogical documentation in due time'. 'Then we have to measure it. It should be measurable. How do we measure it?' she asked. We turned for help to Lean Consultant Karin, who was delivering the training course together with Lean Consultant Monica. Karin suggested that if they reached the goal of having clear pedagogical documentation, they would eventually gain time and the staff would feel job satisfaction. We agreed, but Camilla wondered how it could be measured. Karin proposed that we measure the number of documentations we managed to finish. But she added that we must also find a way to measure job satisfaction. Camilla was thinking out loud: 'How do we measure job satisfaction?' Karin recommended that we have a question in the annual employee survey. Camilla suggested adding to the problem we had formulated in the beginning: To have something to measure, we would add, 'and this, in turn, leads to irritation and stress'. We agreed, and our problem formulation read: 'The problem is that one begins the documentation but does not finish it. It stops, and then one must start over again, and this, in turn, leads to irritation and stress'. Erika finished by saying that we could then measure in the employee survey whether it had become more satisfying.

Now that we had identified our problem, our goal, and how to measure the goal, we were encouraged to start identifying the flow in its *current state*. We positioned yellow Post-its in a flow from left to right on the flipchart-sized paper before us on the table. When we were finished they read:

1 Documentation takes place, writing by hand.
2 Re-type on the computer.
3 No time.
4 Restart (later on).
5 Computer illiteracy.
6 Someone else takes over.
7 Attempting to understand and interpret someone else's handwritten notes.

8   Re-type on the computer.
9   Print.
10  Laminate.
11  Post on the documentation wall [at the preschool].
12  Insert in the documentation folder.
13  Insert in children's portfolios.

We were then ready to determine the flow of the *desired state*. We agreed that the desired state was to remove items 3–8 to make the flow efficient. There were rules for completing a value-stream mapping. The aesthetics of placing the Post-its one after the other on the paper, creating a flow similar to the assembly line is no coincidence. A flow had to be found, and it controlled what was possible for operating within a Lean model.

Lean Consultant Karin stated that we now had two value-stream mappings: the current state and the desired state. She asked us to do a 5 Whys analysis of what was not working. On the table in front of us were stickers in the form of green and red 5-mm-diameter dots. We were to analyse each Post-it in the flow to determine if it brought value to the customer, then analyse the Post-its with red dots, according to the 5 Whys. We started attaching dots on the yellow Post-its: green dots on Post-its 1–2 and 9–13, and red dots on Post-its 3–8 in the flow. We then asked 'Why', five times, and soon agreed that the root of the problem was computer illiteracy and lack of time – without using all of the 5 Whys. Karin was not completely happy with our analysis. She wanted us to continue asking 'Why', and with her help, we came to the realization that the actual root of the problem was the lack of structure and a routine for doing the pedagogical documentation, the lack of opportunities for education in software required for pedagogical documentation, and the lack of responsibility among the staff members to educate themselves on the software.

This outcome gave birth to yet another round of problem identification, a goal, and a way of measuring the results. We completed an *action plan* in the form the A3 Lean tool, on which we wrote the problems of not having a functioning structure and routine for making the pedagogical documentation and educational opportunities and assuring that staff take responsibility for their education. Then we continued to write the background to the problem, the current state, an analysis of the problem, desired state, the plan, an implementation plan, monitoring, and a decision.

Being part of the staff of a preschool a year after taking the Lean coach-training course allowed me to realize that part of our initial analysis was correct, lack of time. The Lean model could not cater to the idea that there was a need to add time rather than find time by making efficient flows, however. Lack of time could not be solved by routines and structures, because the work of preschools was already well organized and well structured. Still, staff members were tempted to hope for a better organization of work through Lean by imagining desired states in which the pedagogical documentation would continuously and regularly appear on the documentation wall, for example.

## A value-stream mapping at Caterpillar Preschool

The municipal management promoted the Lean management model as a way of structuring and organizing the preschool activities to save time, thereby making more time for the children. It was an understandable solution. If there were no room in the budget for more teachers, then the solution may be found in having the staff become more *efficient* – clearly one of the goals for bringing Lean into the municipality. If the preschool staff were to become more efficient, the reasoning went, there would be more time for the users. And if there were more time for the users, the service would automatically become more *qualitative* and thereby result in greater *joy at work*. Many members of the staff and management in the preschool were positive towards Lean, because they hoped that Lean would make more time for them to be the pedagogues they wanted to be. They had no time to evaluate whether the Lean model would be useful for them or not. The municipality wanted them to use Lean, and they attempted to do so.

It was the autumn of 2013, and I was in a value-stream mapping meeting at Caterpillar Preschool in Elm Preschool Unit in my role as an observer. In a conference room in the preschool building, four preschool teachers (Amanda, Erica, Magda, and Elsie), two Lean coaches (Miriam and Berit), and two future Lean coaches (also referred to as 'shadows' because they were shadowing Lean coaches to learn what it meant to be a Lean coach) met in a Lean improvement-group meeting to do a value-stream mapping of the preschool yard.

The value-stream mapping focused on the need to create play areas with clear activities so parents could leave children in an activity rather than with a particular teacher in the morning. There had also been a tendency among the teachers to congregate in the yard, talking amongst each other rather than playing and interacting with the children. The teachers worked to make a flow of the morning so as to come to terms with these problems. Lean Coach Miriam started the day by explaining what Lean was all about. She admitted that she was relatively new to Lean coaching, but explained the philosophy and what it meant to do a value-stream mapping. She ended by saying:

> Let's start with the current state. The Lean idea is to start making the flow of the current state and then make a flow of the desired state. Through this process, you are supposed to identify wastes that need to be rectified.

Amanda, Erica, Magda, and Elsie started to work on the flow. They had four zones in the preschool yard, and they wanted to have clear activities for the children organized into play areas in each zone. Erica tried to make sense of the flow, and wanted to start with the first teacher arriving at the preschool in the morning. Lean Coach Miriam explained that if they had these four zones, they needed four different value streams. Erica responded: 'OK then, we should have four parallel flows. I wonder, should we plan for a Monday [the teachers' meeting day] and a Friday [the teachers' planning day]?' Amanda replied that they needed one for the project days as well. Mondays and Fridays would then be different for staff and children in the yard and on project days when groups moved inside early to start their projects or stayed outside to do the project in the yard. Erica suggested that they could continue the project in just one zone so the teachers and children who didn't work on a project didn't lose several of the zones just because some had started working with the project. Lean Coach Miriam explained that they shouldn't be talking about solutions at this point. The Lean model was strict: Make the flow of the current state and then the desired state. The waste that appears should be handled by creating action plans, preferably involving all staff to arrive at solutions. The idea of involving the entire staff was also part of the ideal of the Lean model, and was based on the assumption that all employees would then feel responsible for continuous improvement.

Miriam took out a roll of brown paper and unrolled it on the table. She explained that they should use the yellow Post-its for each unit of the process, emphasizing that they shouldn't generate solutions at this point; they needed first to identify the units and create the flow. The group started filling out the yellow Post-its. Berit, the other Lean coach, looked at the Post-its and asked if anything happens at Caterpillar Preschool before 7:10 a.m. any day of the week. Erica replied that that has nothing to do with the preschool yard – that they were still in the building at 7:10 a.m. Berit concluded that it might have; she was referring to the Lean idea that every flow unit should be included in the current state, as there might have been a flow unit inside that affected the efficiency in the yard. But Elsie explained that they start at 7:10 a.m. and that only one child came early, so when they listened to the answering machine to determine if any children or staff members were out sick, they could do it while that child was with the teacher opening the preschool. Erica added that one red Post-it has to state that they didn't have enough material in the yard. Amanda added: 'not challenging enough material'. Erica laughed and said that Lean had been introduced precisely because of lack of resources. Amanda asked what kind of explorers the children could be in the yard if there weren't enough material? (The notion of children being explorers is part of the Reggio-Emilia pedagogy and is also present in the Curriculum.) They could dig in the sandbox and swing on the swing, Amanda continued: 'Inside we think about how they can be explorers, but we don't do it in the yard. We need to do that outside as well'.

Elsie agreed that they also needed to think about how the children could be explorers outside. She explained that they could think of what they did in the *construction* play area inside: When the children started to build something, the teachers treated what the children had built as the start of something that could be further explored. But she also added that children who came early were not especially alert and may not want to start exploring. Amanda agreed, but said that they should have books too, for the children who are tired. She added: 'Now I'm going to write something that I don't like, and that is "calm activities", because it implies not being active'.

The teachers continued to discuss the activities they wanted to have in the yard and how all the teachers could be inspired, in turn, to inspire the children to become explorers. Amanda mentioned the fact that sand also could be mathematical – that filling a bucket with sand could be turned into a mathematics lesson. She also mentioned hanging a picture that would inspire the children. She had been at a *pedagogical cafe* arranged by the municipality and the presenter described how she had hung pictures of children building a volcano and how these pictures had inspired the other children. They continued with suggestions of possible activities, while the Lean coaches continued to try to make them find the flow units in the flow, focusing on time slots, the number of staff members, and routines, instead of solutions.

When they had managed to fill the brown paper with yellow Post-its representing flow units, Lean Coach Miriam wanted them to make the desired state. They should use red Post-its when they found a problem and green if a quick solution could be found – a waste that could be eliminated immediately. Erica wondered if that would not be a waste of time. Miriam asked if they really wanted to skip a stage in the process – that it's good if they do the value-stream mapping according to Lean, which, in a way, is ironic, given that Lean is all about eliminating waste. 'Okay, but how will we do that? Should we put a lot of green Post-its here?' Erica pointed at the brown paper and the yellow Post-it flow. Miriam said that they could make another row with the desired state.

We broke for lunch at that point, but when we returned, Erica again argued that they already knew what they wanted to change – that they wanted to make the action plans today:

> We need two action plans, one for the structure and one for the activities. The structure is the foundation for how it will work and the activities part is more about what we will do, how it is connected to the Curriculum, and the preschool's values and perspective on children. But then we might need several action plans for the activities?

Miriam wondered if the teachers would like to see an action plan. She gave them an *A4* (printed on A4 paper) document that included such headings as Goal, Responsible, Evaluation. Erica read the headings and became excited: 'Oh, this exactly what we've been talking about'. Miriam reminded them that they shouldn't get involved in that now. First they had to complete the desired state. Erica said: 'Okay, let's do our dream state first'. A discussion started on how to make the dream state. Where should the green Post-its go? Miriam asked everyone to take a deep breath. She said that they were expected to do this tomorrow, so they had time.

Erica asked Elsie to write. Elsie wrote: '7:30: Pedagogue One takes out material and brings it to Zone 4, together with the children'. Amanda clarified that it was necessary for them to take out material for all four zones of the yard, because it was important that there be things to do when they opened up the other three zones when all the children had arrived. Magda noted that they needed to go over the material to see what they had before they could make the activities' guide: 'But it shouldn't take long. We would need an afternoon'. Erica suggested that they could have ready-made activity boxes, and Amanda reminded them that they had tried this before and it hadn't worked. Magda argued that they all had to be responsible for the material. Miriam tried to get them back to Lean and asked if they had done the Lean 5S: *Sort, Set in order, Shine, Standardize,* and *Sustain the practice.*

Erica ignored Miriam and said that if they had material and activities, many of the problems they had identified would be sorted out – problems such as teachers congregating together in the yard. Lean Coach Berit asked them to go back a few steps and return to drawing up the desired state: 'How many play areas should you start to make ready at 7:30?' Erica answered that all five play areas had to be made ready. Berit asked if they have staff for all five play areas? Erica replied that they do by 8:15 a.m. Amanda clarified that some of the play areas needed a teacher supervising, but other areas needed only to be on display, and they would entice the children to interact with them. They continue to talk about the other zones. Erica said: 'Do we all agree that we want clear activities in Zone 4 at 9 o'clock? And then we clean up and eat fruit. And in the meantime, one teacher is responsible for preparing the other zones'. Everyone agreed.

The teachers talked about what they could do in the other zones. Elsie suggested that they could make drawings on the asphalt. Erica responded that it had derailed the last time they tried that when the children started to draw on the wall instead of the asphalt. Then Magda remembered that she was drawing with some children on the asphalt and behind her back there were children drawing on the wall. Lean Coach Berit again tried to bring everyone back to the Lean exercise, making them focus on the desired state rather than generating solutions. Erica looked at the Post-its and concluded that they had finished with the cleaning up and the fruit, and now they needed to think about the zones. 'What should they do in what zone?' They started talking about which zone was which, and what they should include. Berit again tried to remind them to return to the flow.

This back and forth continued, during which the teachers wanted to discuss ways of improving the activities of the preschool, and the Lean coaches attempted to bring them back to the flow, the structure of the process – the focus of Lean. The logic of the Lean model did not fit what the teachers wanted to work on. They already had the structure. The problem was clear activities, not identified value-added and non-value-added time in a flow, and this was not a problem that Lean could help solve because of its focus on identifying wastes that disturbed the efficiency of the flow.

## Conclusion: the Lean smoothing machine

As a socially produced smoothing machine, Lean works at many levels, smoothing the surfaces between flow units on the assembly line. Lean smooths flow units by ensuring that the cycle time on the workstation – inserting one piece of the car into another – is flowing smoothly. Lean smooths ideas and tools by incorporating 8 wastes in the model designed to reduce unnecessary movement and waiting. Lean smooths tools and work units by keeping standard inventory to a minimum at the flow units and smooths work processes through the work sequence. Lean means standardization and bureaucratization at the micro level, smoothing all surfaces among ideas, tools, and activities, ensuring that there no waste is left to polish and coat.

Waste has a specific meaning in the Lean model, based upon what is considered the problem of 'not adding value' to the perceived customer. On the assembly line, it means that all movements and any waiting time not adding value is considered waste. It is based on the elimination of movements to save time. In preschools, there is no waste in movements or waiting in interaction with the children. All occasions can be made, even should be made, into pedagogical moments. What would be waste on the assembly line – stopping the flow – would be care and pedagogy in preschools. What could be considered waste in a preschool environment would, for example, be teachers congregating in the yard, talking to each other rather than playing and interacting with the children. But this could not be solved by doing a value-stream mapping. For one thing, the so-called waste was already identified, and for another thing, there was no line that could be smoothed to solve this problem.

What could be considered waste in a preschool environment would be the technologies of convenience, as in the modern household; but not even that is true, because preschool teachers were masters of making what others would consider waste into pedagogical material: milk cartons, toilet rolls, and bottle caps. Even recycling became a pedagogical moment, walking with the 1- to 2-year-olds to the recycling station nearby to teach them about recycling. In this way, making value out of waste.

In the Lean model, waste has a performative role, in that markings and cuts considered waste should be ground, coated, and aligned. The goal of the Lean smoothing machine is finding and polishing the breaks, so that waste is turned into shiny surfaces blending in. The break between Lean and the preschool world was impossible to grind, polish, and blend, however. There is no smoothing machine that can align and smooth between Lean and preschool care and pedagogy.

# References

Bauman, Zygmunt (2001), 'Excess: An obituary', *Parallax*, 7 (1), 85–91.
Bogard, William (2000), 'Smoothing machines and the constitution of society', *Cultural Studies*, 14 (2), 269–294.
Cresswell, Tim (2006), *On the move: Mobility in the modern western world* (New York: Routledge).
Deleuze, Gilles and Guattari, Félix (1987), *A thousand plateaus: Capitalism and schizophrenia* (Minneapolis: University of Minnesota Press).
Douglas, Mary (1966 [1991]), *Purity and danger: An analysis of the concepts of pollution and taboo* (London: Routledge).
Frow, John (2003), 'Invidious distinction: Waste, difference, and classy staff', in Gay Hawkins and Stephen Muecke (eds.), *Culture and waste: The creation and destruction of value* (Lanham: Rowman & Littlefield).
Hawkins, Gay (2006), *The ethics of waste: How we relate to rubbish* (Lanham: Rowman & Littlefield).
Ingold, Tim (2007 [2016]), *Lines: A brief history* (London: Routledge).
Liker, Jeffrey K. (2004), *The Toyota way: 14 management principles from the world's greatest manufacturer* (London: McGraw-Hill).
Mauss, Marcel (1925 [2002]), *The gift: The form and reason for exchange in archaic societies* (London: Routledge).
Modig, Niklas and Åhlström, Pär (2012), *This is lean: Resolving the efficiency paradox* (Stockholm: Rheologica Publishing).
Ohno, Taiichi (1988), *Toyota production system: Beyond large-scale production* (London: CRC Press).
Peck, Jamie and Theodore, Nik (2015a), *Fast policy: Experimental statecraft at the thresholds of neoliberalism* (Minneapolis: University of Minnesota Press).
———— (2015b), 'Paying for good behavior: Cash transfer policies in the wild', in Ananya Roy and Emma Shaw Crane (eds.), *Territories of poverty: Rethinking north and south* (Athens: University of Georgia Press).
Radnor, Zoe J., Holweg, Matthias, and Waring, Justin (2012), 'Lean in healthcare: The unfilled promise?', *Social Science & Medicine*, 74 (3), 364–371.
Rosa, Hartmut (2017), 'De-synchronization, dynamic stabilization, dispositional squeeze', in Judy Wajcman and Nigel Dodd (eds.), *The sociology of speed: Digital, organizational, and social temporalities* (Oxford: Oxford University Press), 25–41.
Salazar, Noel B. and Jayaram, Kiran (2016), *Keywords of mobility: Critical engagements* (Oxford, UK: Berghahn Books).
Strasser, Susan (1999), *Waste and want: A social history of trash* (New York: Holt Paperbacks).
Taylor, Frederick Winslow (1911 [2006]), *The principles of scientific management* (Middlesex: The Echo Library).
Thompson, Michael (1979 [2017]), *Rubbish theory: The creation and destruction of value, new edition* (Oxford: Pluto Press).
Veblen, Thorstein (1899 [1932]), *The theory of the leisure class: An economic study of institutions* (New York: Vanguard).
Woolgar, Steve and Neyland, Daniel (2013), *Mundane governance: Ontology and accountability* (Oxford: Oxford University Press).
Womack, James P. and Jones, Daniel T. (1996), *Lean thinking: Banish waster and create wealth in your corporation* (New York: Simon & Schuster).

# Chapter 6

# Plan
## Hoping for an efficient future

It was the autumn of 2012, and I was participating in a three-day Lean coach-training course held in the municipality where I was performing my preschool fieldwork. My goal was to learn about Lean and how it was being taught in the municipality. We were seated at tables for four, where a flipchart-sized paper lay. Lean Consultant Karin, who was giving the course, pointed to the large sheet of paper and explained that it was supposed to typify Lean's problem-solving document, which is known merely by its paper size: *A3*. The flipchart-sized paper represented a chart that featured nine labelled cells (see Table 6.1).

Karin presented the chart cell by cell, explaining what should be written under each heading: 'First, you have to articulate the problem'. The problem-solving A3 document was the result of identified waste in such areas as value-stream mapping, explained in Chapter 5. Elimination of the waste had to be communicated through an A3 report, which should include the *current state* of the work process and an *analysis of the problem* on the left-hand side of the paper. When analysing the problem, we should remember to use the *5 Whys* to get to the root of the problem.

The right-hand side of the paper should comprise an *action plan* for eliminating the waste, in order to achieve the *desired state*. The desired state should be clearly stated in the 'Desired state' cell, along with a statement about what things would be like when that state is reached: 'What are the goals and what are the effects?' The four cells below Desired state in the action plan outline the PDCA process, one per cell: following the Deming's cycle of *Plan, Do, Check,* and *Act*. Karin drew a circle on paper, dividing it into four pieces, writing a letter in each piece: P, D, C, A. She explained: 'This is the PDCA Cycle'. The A3 document should include all the elements of the PDCA cycle. The Plan should include a *project plan* of the activities required and what they would cost. The Do part should include an *implementation plan* of the steps to be taken, the order in which they were to be taken, who was responsible, and when it would be finished. Check should state how to measure and evaluate whether the action would achieve the desired state. When it was determined that the desired state was reached, the implementation should be final and possibly standardized.

*Table 6.1* 'A3' problem-solving document

| Problem | Desired state: |
|---|---|
| Background | Plan – project plan |
| Current state | Do – implementation plan |
| Analysis of the problem | Check – monitor and evaluate |
|  | Act |

As Lean coaches, we were taught that we would first have to help the group of staff members we were working with to write an A3 and then ensure that they had an action plan that covered the points in the PDC part of the process before they could turn to Act. Karin explained that this was a slow process; it might be six months before they would come to Act. During the PD and C parts of the process, she said, all staff members were welcome to provide their viewpoints, but when they turned to Act, it was no longer the time to have opinions and make changes; it was time to Act on the decision. She said that it was critical that we understand this cycle, that we should put a picture of the PDCA Cycle in the workplace and explain that during the PDC period the opinions of every colleague were of interest, although during the Do phase the plan should be tried before opinions were raised. But when A arrived, everyone was required to support it, because the time had come to do as prescribed. She ended by saying that it was important to set dates in the circle so that staff always knew which phase they were in.

This chapter investigates plans and planning in preschools. It focuses on the hope produced by the Lean action plan of turning current states into desired states. The notion of a plan has a temporal aspect, promising something for the future. In this way, it is intimately connected to hope. Plans can control, oppress, change, or improve, but inherent in plans is the hope for a better future for someone or something, even if it is in the name of oppression. In this chapter, I discuss the role of plans, as promises for the future are made (Abram and Weszkalnys 2013). The main focus is on the affective and performative role played by plans in the Lean model, and on the way they relate to preschools. How are plans and planning performed in the Lean model and in preschools? What hopes do they project? How do Lean plans operate in preschools?

The outline of this chapter reflects the fact that implementing Lean in preschools requires that it be added to the workload involved in childcare and in the education of the children. I highlight the difficulties of fitting Lean into the daily activities of Swedish preschools by moving back and forth between the Lean model and the everyday life of the preschool, demonstrating the tensions among the dispositions of the model, the dispositions of preschool work, and the requirements of preschool work. In first part of the chapter, I present research on planning and hope. In the following section, I describe how plans and planning are performed and used in the Lean model. I then turn to what planning means and how it is performed in preschools. The final two sections in the chapter focus on Lean plans in preschools. In the Conclusion section, I contend that Lean began to work as deception (Lashaw 2008), making an improbable future believable and keeping rebellion against savings and shortage of staff at arm's length.

## Plans and the hope for a better future

In the area of urban and spatial planning, planning and plans are connected primarily to public policy. It is about development: organizing welfare and progress and improving conditions of housing and welfare institutions for the future (Robertson 1984). Planning is formed around rational logic, whereby an objective is to be fulfilled through programmes, action plans, and a specific action that can be monitored if the goal is met (Head and Alford 2015). It is based on the assumption 'that each public organization has settled goals, a supportive political environment, and control over the resources and capabilities necessary to deliver on the goals' (Head and Alford 2015: 720). But as Rittel and Webber (1973) have noted, planners must deal with societal problems – what they call 'wicked problems', because these problems are always unique, that there is seldom one solution, and that there is no room for trial and error. Plans provide the promise of a better future, a transition from the current state to a desired state (Abram and Weszkalnys 2013). But rather than treating plans as blueprints for the future, Abram and Weszkalnys ask us to investigate what plans do, what kind of work they perform.

The 'elusive promise' (Abram and Weszkalnys 2013) of plans project an ideal rather than portray a possible achieved outcome that is never really possible to complete. Yet even if the promise is not fulfilled, the promise itself fulfils a role (Abram and Weszkalnys 2013). Anderson (2006) draws attention to affect in relation to planning and emphasizes the importance of affective responses to the hope that is inherent in plans. Policy and plans are animated by elusive promises and by affectivity, often to maintain and generate hope (Anderson and Holden 2008). The affective powers of hope work as a 'resource affect' (Weszkalnys 2016) for plans.

Like plans, hope is intimately connected to the future, to the 'not-yet-conscious' (Bloch 1959 [1986]). Bloch's not-yet-conscious is a response to Freud's ideas of the unconscious, in which he emphasized the latent ability of humans to anticipate that which is yet to be articulated. In contrast to Freud's night dreams, Bloch compares hope to a daydream, as in dreaming forward, in his understanding of hope as a subjective resource for political action. There has been renewed scholarly interest in hope as a subjective resource for political action. Harvey (2000) argues that we must find a space for the 'optimism of the intellect'. He paraphrases Antonio Gramsci (1971), connecting Gramsci's terms 'pessimism of the intellect' and 'optimism of the will' to the notion of hope. Harvey (2000) concludes that optimism of the will is not enough. It is through 'optimism of the intellect' that we can pursue truly progressive policies and create an alternative to neoliberal ideals. Appadurai (2013) emphasizes the need to bring back the modern project as a political project. He argues that the utopian dimension of modernity gives hope for a better future, for a better, more equal world. In the modern project, he contends, there is a belief in social development, with such values as fairness, rationality, freedom, and participation.

Bloch's phenomenology of hope has been further explored by Dodd (2004), who emphasized the consciousness of the temporality of the present moment when analysing hope. He suggests that hope can also consist of something that may never come about, thus putting hope in the present, as a future already in place. In this way, hope may work as a form of deception that makes an improbable future believable: 'Progress, in other words, is experienced as imminence' (Lashaw 2008: 110). Plans give hope and hope has agentic powers, Lashaw maintains; it heightens people's ability to tolerate suffering because of a better, imagined future. It points to the dark side of planning and using plans for social control and oppression of citizenry (Abram and Weszkalnys 2013; Yiftachel 1998), as colonial planning has done for centuries in controlling indigenous people (Porter 2010). Abram and Weszkalnys (2013) write about the colonializing effects of planning in the name of public good, as states try to govern more people and things.

In this chapter, I treat hope and plans as an ethnographic category for critical analysis (cf. Kleist and Jansen 2016). I am interested in the agentic powers of hope in creating imagined futures when Lean plans are made and in the colonializing effects of Lean plans in preschools. It is the performative role of plans and their ability to provoke affective responses that is investigated here in relation to Lean and the organization of preschools. The main focus is what plans and hope *do* in preschools.

## Action plans and PDCA cycles

The A3 document is a critical tool in the Lean toolbox, to be used when waste is identified as requiring elimination. It should include all the important data in a problem-solving process by documenting the current situation, determining the root cause of the problem, analysing the problem and the desired state, suggesting other solutions, and recommending solutions for an action plan (Liker 2004). A3 paper was used because it was the largest paper that could fit in a fax machine at the time of its invention (Liker 2004). The problem-solving A3 document should be able to stand alone, because it includes all necessary information, communicates the required improvements visually, and needs no verbal presentation. The theory is that too many words bore people, and that lengthy reports are a waste of time (Liker 2004). In fact, the ultimate goal was to have the problem-solving document printed on the smaller A4 paper (Liker 2004).

Although the A3 document was based on Deming's PDCA (Womack et al. 1990), it started one step before Plan, as it included the current state and the policies and reasons for the current state (Liker 2004). In the automotive industry that could be a flow on the assembly line that had identified a number of wastes in the value-stream mapping process of identifying the current state and the desired state. The waste needed to be described on the A3, which included an action plan for reaching the desired state. The P demanded a project plan, D an implementation plan, and C a measurable goal, in order to act on the desired state of A. The PDCA Cycle is an improvement wheel, which should be used to strive for continuous improvement – in Lean terms, greater efficiency. It should be used as a way of forward motion and continuous learning (Shook 1997). The A3 problem-solving document and the PDCA cycle are cornerstones of Lean, providing tools for the process of turning plans into action in the spirit of continuous improvement – verifying that any waste that does not add value is eliminated (Liker 2004).

Thus Lean is always future oriented. It is about making continuous improvement with the goal of having a more rational, efficient future. Efficiency requires that the desired state be reached. And in the name of continuous improvement, there is always another desired state around the corner, urging another PDCA cycle. The A3 problem-solving document, including the action plan, emphasizes the desired future. The very existence of the A3 document and the action plan evokes affective responses of hope for a better, more rational, and efficient future.

## Planning occurring on the fly

Preschool planning involves another type of planning for action, having to do with co-ordination between divisions and staff and with planning for pedagogical activities. It evokes another type of future and another type of hope, other than the hope for Lean efficiency. Preschool planning and co-ordination took place in different meetings (see also Chapter 3). In Birch Preschool Unit, which is the focus of this section, management planning ensured that operational plans were written and municipal policies were followed – were performed in the management group meeting consisting of Unit Head Christina, Pedagogist Lovisa, and the preschool heads of the four preschools: Bumblebee, Spider, Grasshopper, and Cricket. Management group planning involved overarching planning following four overlapping 'years': the *Organizational year*, the *Systematic quality work year*, the *Pedagogical year*, and the *Parental collaboration year*. Birch Preschool Unit used a so-called *årshjul* (wheel of the year) for each of these four years, documenting what needed to be done each month – systematic quality work or pedagogical activities, for example.

The preschool heads – in this case Sigrid of Bumblebee Preschool – brought information from the management meetings to the weekly meetings. There were four divisions in Bumblebee Preschool, and the preschool head and the four division heads met weekly to plan and co-ordinate, making sure that there were enough staff in each division to attend meetings if sickness were to cause understaffing. Apart from planning and organizing the week, the weekly meetings of the heads also concerned issues specific to their preschool – issues involving the whole school that they should bring up at the *APT* (workplace) meeting: changing routines, planning a reorganizing of the schoolyard, or calling for a parental meeting. The divisions had their own planning meetings, in which the week was planned and co-ordinated in detail, including such issues as which of the children would present their project during circle time or where they would go for an excursion that week.

It was the autumn of 2013, and I arrived at Bumblebee Preschool just before 8:00 a.m. I was joining one of the four divisions in Bumblebee for its weekly meeting – in this case the teachers working with the 2- to 3-year-olds. Even though I worked as a staff member at the time, I was primarily an observer in these meetings. Louise, Ingrid, Karla, and I gathered behind Olga, who was seated in front of the computer in the staff room. Division Head Karla started by informing us that she and Preschool Head Sigrid had redone the work schedule for the preschool and wondered if everyone had time to have a look. Everyone nodded, but Olga pointed out that she had been scheduled for 15 minutes more than her working hours, a situation that needed to be changed. Karla agreed and said that she was already onto it. We then turned to the *pedagogical documentation*. Olga had prepared documentation that they were to discuss, with the goal of reaching agreement on how to present the documentations of the on-going pedagogical project with sand, on the pedagogical documentation wall in the preschool. As described in Chapter 3, each child had brought a box of sand to the preschool, and, depending on their age, worked with the sand project differently. Older children showed the other children on a map where they had found their sand, told the others about it, and passed it around for comment from the other children. The 2- to 3-year-olds, who had collected their sand nearby, were taken to that location where they all collected more sand. This process made it easier for the children to understand what the project was about and allowed children who weren't yet verbal to do something physical by collecting sand.

The children's conversation about and actions with the sand were documented in the pedagogical documentation, and the discussion today was how to present all of that on the pedagogical documentation wall. Olga showed us the PowerPoint she had made of 2-year-old Vilma's sand presentation after they had been to the place where Vilma had collected the sand. The project was divided into two stages: They went to the location of Vilma's sand collection, then, back at the preschool, the children reflected on the excursion with the help of photographs that Olga had taken as they collected the sand. Olga had first written the text and then added some pictures, but she wondered if this was how the documentation should best be presented. When finished, it should be placed on the pedagogical documentation wall in the preschool division for parents and children to see. Louise suggested that they first needed a text about the sand project. Ingrid agreed, saying that she thought they should begin with an introduction followed by documentations of each child's sand project.

Together we looked through the pictures that Olga had taken during the reflection with Vilma and the other children. We found a photograph in which Vilma was seated on a chair, telling the other children – with the help of the teacher – about what she had shown them at her sand location. Olga pointed out that it felt good that Vilma was seated in a chair and the others were seated on the floor when they were looking at the photographs. It helped to place the focus on Vilma and her sand place. Karla added that she had seen that 2-year-old Maja did the same when they were talking about her sand. 'Yes', Louise added, 'They do it outside as well [in the schoolyard]'. Ingrid then told us that she had drawn up a model at home last night: 'I have it on an USB stick. Should I show it to you?' 'Yes please;' answered Olga. 'I can move'. She turned the computer over to Ingrid, who sat down and showed her Power-Point. Ingrid had drawn a square in the upper right-hand corner of the picture where she had written:

> **Focus question:** What do you want to show at the place where you found your sand?
> **Mission:** To find the place where the sand was collected, and then, all together, fill a new box of sand to bring to the preschool.
> **Purpose:** [which she had left blank]

The group agreed with her ideas. The focus of the exercise was to document what the children wanted to show at the place they had collected the sand. Ingrid asked what design they wanted. Should there be one or two sections of text? Should they have one or more photographs? Karla said that they shouldn't have too many pictures, because there wouldn't be room on the documentation wall. She wondered how it was done in the previous year, and Olga informed us that they had had one page of text and then two photos, but that had taken a great deal of room. They agreed the child should choose one photo taken when they visited the location of the sand. Louise said that it wouldn't be possible to print all the photos for the child to choose from, so the choice would have to be made from the computer. Olga objected that it would be easier for the child if they printed a number of photos. Louise disagreed: 'But can't they choose from the computer?' Ingrid agreed with Olga, and said that if they placed all the photographs on the floor, it would become part of the children's reflection. Olga agreed, adding that she also thought of it as part of the reflection with the children.

Karla brought the group back to the 'Purpose' written in the box suggested by Ingrid, noting that it should say something from the Preschool Curriculum. Olga, who thought that Ingrid's model was better, asked if they all had agreed with Ingrid. They all did, but Karla again reminded everyone that they needed to have a purpose connected to the Curriculum. Olga and Louise were teacher assistants, not university-educated preschool teachers, but Karla and Ingrid were, and it was their responsibility to guarantee that the Preschool Curriculum was followed. In fact, they were responsible for following what was inscribed in the Curriculum (Preschool Curriculum 2011), which would explain Karla's constant reminders. Karla concluded that she could look through the Curriculum to find a good purpose and put it on the PowerPoint. She confirmed that we had agreed on a model for the pedagogical documentation.

Division Head Karla moved the discussion forward by asking how we should plan for the day. Olga suggested that she and Ingrid would bring in a group of children today to reflect. Ingrid agreed, but then asked who would make an excursion to a new sand place today. Karla wanted to go, but she wanted to have someone with her who had been at a sand place before, because she hadn't had time to do it before. Olga changed her mind and said that she could join Karla. Ingrid then concluded that she and Louise would bring a group of children inside to reflect on the photos and what 2-year-old Denise had said that she wanted to show from an earlier excursion. I ended up joining Karla and Olga.

Preschool planning involves the co-ordination of schedules, the presentation of pedagogical documentation on the documentation wall, or co-ordination of the day. Preschool planning involves a great deal of co-ordination because there always have to be teachers present taking care of and educating children. These are plans for co-ordination – not plans for Lean efficiency. Planning for the pedagogical documentation focuses on fair and consistent presentations on the documentation wall – all the children's sand projects are represented in the same way, for instance. Co-ordination of the day is a form of instant planning that has to do with the near future and must occur on the fly. In that sense, it is not a visionary future, but a real future. This type of near-future planning fits well in an organization in which children or teachers are off sick at the last moment, quickly changing long-term plans.

## Trying to turn Lean plans into action 1

Lean planning in preschools was undertaken to create a vision for the future – a desired state – like pedagogical documentation continuously and regularly appearing on the pedagogical documentation wall. Lean promised that this would be possible if everyone worked towards the desired state and turned plans into actions. A group of teachers at Bumblebee Preschool had met in an improvement-group meeting to complete a value-stream mapping. They formulated an action plan to decide how much of their planning time should be allotted to pedagogical documentation. *Planning time* in preschools is also known as childfree time – the working time that employees are allotted for planning, rearranging the preschool, and participating in meetings or any work that does not include childcare and children's education. University-degree preschool teachers were given 4 hours a week, and teacher assistants with a high school degree in childcare and non-certified teachers had 3 hours a week. Some of the teachers, I was told, did not use all of their allotted time. But most of them did. And they also had to bank their planning time so they would have enough time for semi-annual teacher-parent conferences and teacher-parent meetings.

The *A3* document and the Lean action plan document layout may look different, depending on the amount of effort that had been put into the design. Some are more elaborate, with colours and company logos, whereas others, like the one used by the teachers at Bumblebee Preschool, had more of a homemade look. The municipality worked with an action plan document, not including the *current state*, which according to Lean guru Liker (2004) should be included for it to be a proper A3 document. The municipality's Lean action plan document was also printed on A4 paper, which would have pleased Liker, as this was the eventual goal of the A3 problem-solving document. The A4 action plan included the following headings from the top to the bottom and left to right.

> What do we want to achieve? *Objective*
> How will it be when we have reached the objective? *Measure and criteria for good quality within the activity*
> What do we need to do to achieve the objective?
> Time plan
> How and when will we control the result? *Evaluation method*
> Who will carry out the activity and who will we need support from?
> Who is responsible for the activity?
>
> > 30-day follow-up
> > 60-day follow-up
> > 90-day follow-up

In Bumblebee Preschool, there was a problem with finishing pedagogical documentation, and it seemed to be a problem in preschools in general, as it also appeared in the Lean coach-training course. When doing a Lean value-stream mapping of the pedagogical documentation process, the group of teachers in the Lean improvement-group had decided that the objective was to have pedagogical documentation continuously and regularly appearing on the pedagogical documentation wall. They had also come up with the solution of allotting a number of hours of teachers' planning time, which they had written in the column entitled 'What do we need to do to achieve the objective?' A working group had merely to decide how many hours should be allocated to planning time. It made sense to allot a number of hours, because it would be easy to measure in Lean terms. Each staff member had to report the number of hours used for planning time each month. According to Lean logic, if a certain number of hours were allotted to pedagogical documentation, then the pedagogical documentation would be finished and would continuously and regularly appear on the documentation wall. In the action plan, the teachers had written that when the goal was reached: 'There would be documentation presented on the pedagogical documentation wall in the preschool every week, ensuring that pedagogical documentation becomes the work tool it is meant to be'. The action plan stated that Unit Head Christina was responsible, and that she and Preschool Head Sigrid needed to decide only the number of hours, to be evaluated at the 30-day, 60-day, and 90-day follow-ups, to assure that they would reach the Act stage in the PDCA Cycle.

At first glance, it seemed like a clear-cut, easily written action plan. It was not as easy to turn it into action, however. At the 30-day follow-up in the autumn of 2013, Lean Coach Margaret informed the Bumblebee Preschool staff that they were going through the action plans to determine if they were green, yellow, or red. Lean Coach Jennifer read 'appoint a working group'; it was green: 'Decide how much of the planning time should be devoted to pedagogical documentation weekly. Have you done that?' Unit Head Christina said that they weren't finished. 'We talked about 1-1/2 hours, but then we revised. No, we aren't ready yet'. Lean Coach Margaret asked: 'Do you have a new timetable for that?' And Lina, one of the teachers, answered, 'No'. Christina elaborated on her point: There were some things that needed to be considered. Another teacher, Rosanna, asked if they hadn't talked about 3 hours, and Lina replied that they had talked about a maximum of 3 hours.

Unit Head Christina informed the coaches that the preschool teachers had more planning hours allotted to them than the teacher assistants did, and if the group consisted of two preschool teachers or one preschool teacher and one teacher assistant, they would have different numbers of planning hours. She said that they had talked in the management group about a quota system in relation to the number of children and ended by saying that she thought that that would be a better system. Rosanna disagreed, saying that they had been talking about having a minimum of 1 and a maximum of 3 hours. Hilda, a teacher, asked if this was the system that they should try now: 1–3 hours? Rosanna corrected her, saying that she thought it was counted on the *parpedagog* (pedagogical pair: The teachers organized their work so that they worked in pairs with the children). Hilda agreed: 'Yes, of course. I meant pedagogical pair'. Unit Head Christina said quickly: 'Good, then we can mark it green'. Rosa, another teacher, disagreed, saying that she works with older children and that requires much more documentation, because the children talked and discussed things: 'We would never be able to finish if we can use only three hours'. Christina responded that we had talked about it and had agreed that it was possible to do pedagogical documentation while caring for the older children, because they were not in constant need of supervision. 'And then it's not planning time, because then you're with the children', Christina added.

Lina, a teacher, said that when we checked, most of us didn't use more than 3 hours anyway. Christina replied that maybe we can try it, and then we can return to discuss it at the 60-day follow-up: 'I see that you shake your head, Rosa', she added. Lean Coach Margaret asked if they should return the action plan to Lean colour yellow. Christina replied that they could try to document how it turns out. Nora, another teacher, agreed with Rosa, saying that it took one hour to write just one documentation. Lean Coach Margaret interrupted the flow of the conversation by saying that this was a follow-up meeting and the on-going discussion was one that they needed to have amongst themselves. Lean Coach Josefine said 'We leave it yellow'. Margaret and Josefine left the meeting, but the discussion regarding the hours continued. Unit Head Christina said: 'But should we have a minimum of three hours instead?' Lina said that then it could be a minimum of 3 hours and a maximum of 4? Hilda agreed, saying, 'Let's try and then evaluate'. Lina agreed: 'Yes, let's try'.

Lean Coach Margaret began the 60-day follow-up by saying that they needed to go through the action plans marked yellow that day. Lina informed the coaches that the last time they had written 1–3 hours for planning time devoted to pedagogical documentation, but that they had later decided 3–4 hours per pedagogical pair. Margaret confirmed, saying that they were supposed to test this option until today and finished by asking everyone how it had worked out. Ingrid answered that she thought it had worked well – that she had used about that much time – and Hilda said that it had helped her prioritize. Lean Coach Josefine added that one of the points with the action plan was to highlight how much time was spent. Now that they had turned the action plan into Do, it was marked green on the monitoring document.

At the 90-day follow-up, Lean Coach Josefine asked if they had evaluated how it worked to devote 3–4 hours to pedagogical documentation. 'Is it something that you will continue with?' Hilda answered that they would continue to work with that model, but that it had not always turned out that way. Lina said that no one was against it at the 60-day follow-up: 'But do we think it's enough time?' Rosanna said that it was enough if they could do some of it while caring for the children. Ulrika, a teacher, said that she had to do some of it while taking care of the children or she wouldn't have had time to go to her network meetings. Unit Head Christina responded that it was not forbidden to do document pedagogical documentation while caring for the children and that it could also be pedagogical to do it with the children. Adrienne, yet another teacher, said that we could have 3–4 hours as an objective. Susann, another teacher, agreed that it could be our intention.

The action plan for deciding how much time should be dedicated to pedagogical documentation so that pedagogical documentation would appear continuously and regularly on the documentation wall had already met with problems in the Do phase. Even though the staff finally agreed on the number of hours, the actual doing was merely an intention rather than an action. The realities of preschools, with at least one staff member – and often two or three – off sick or home with their own sick children,[1] absent for training, or in a meeting, and with a budget that did not always allow for substitutes, would ensure that this intention remained an intention. In this way, the action plan simultaneously produced hope and a constant feeling of failure.

## Trying to turn Lean plans into action II

A group of teachers responsible for turning an action plan for the schoolyard into action met in the basement of Ladybug Preschool in the autumn of 2013. Carolina began the discussion by asking if they could start by talking about the outer yard, because she needed to leave early. She said that she wanted to discuss the *runners* first, though. The runners, who were in charge of greeting parents and children, taking children to the bathroom in the morning, and helping other teachers who were responsible for play, were supposed to wear yellow vests so parents and children could identify them when they arrived in the morning. The runner assignment circulated among the teachers. Carolina said that they needed a specific place to keep the vests because yesterday they had spent a long time looking for them, and one of the vests was still missing. She suggested that they should hang them on the clothes hanger by the entrance to the kitchen. They decided to do that and started to talk about the outer part of the yard, where the older children were; the younger children were in the smaller inner part.

'What have we done?' Carolina read the minutes from the last meeting. Nils said, laughing: 'Some inventory has been done – that is, we have looked in the boxes in the yard'. Carolina, trying to be a bit more serious, said that they had started to make picture tags for what was – or rather what should be – in the boxes and hung them above the boxes. Camilla asked if the tags shouldn't be on the boxes. Carolina said that she hadn't even thought about it, but wouldn't the children tear them off if they were on the box? The teachers had to think

---

1 In the Swedish social insurance system, children's caregivers are financially compensated if they miss work because they need to be home with a sick child. This temporary parental leave is based on the caregiver's income. In 2018, caregivers receive 80 per cent of their salary up to a maximum of 37,919 SEK (~ 3,792 EUR; ~ 4,339 USD) per month.

of the smaller children who might tear the pictures off, but they also wanted to make sure the older children, who were helping to put things away as part of pedagogy, could see the pictures and know what should be put where.

Tora said that they also talked about doing a drawing for what should be where – a drawing that should be placed in the storage house in the yard. Nils exclaimed: 'Oh, I should have done that already. But I haven't. I will!' Tora noted that it could benefit from being extremely well defined and precise. Carolina continued with the minutes and concluded they had managed to fix the box that didn't have a lid: 'I think everyone has been looking at that box, but has done nothing. Now, Ingrid and I have fixed it'. Carolina continued:

> Then even if we have posted notes, it's not always the stuff that should be in the box that is in it. We need to be more meticulous when we put back the toys and stuff, so it ends up in the right box.

Nils suggested that they should send a 'scolding mail' to everyone. Carolina went on to say that they needed more storage boxes. Nils informed us that the ones they have were made of wood, but that maybe they shouldn't have those made of wood, because they rot: 'Is it possible to have some other kind of material?' 'Plastic', suggested Carolina. 'Or concrete', laughed Camilla.

Carolina returned to the minutes and reminded everyone about tidying. She noted that the current practice was to start tidying the yard furthest away and then all the children ended up in the atelier or with the bicycles because there weren't enough things for the children to do while the yard was being tidied. Carolina wanted it to be the other way around, suggesting that they leave until last the 40-cm$^3$ plastic cubes that the children could move around, climb on, and pile up, so the children had something to do. Tora said that that sounded like a good idea, but that they had to tell Lauren, who was responsible for the inner part of the yard. Nils laughed and said that he can formulate it so that all the responsibility becomes Lauren's. Carolina wanted to finish so she could leave and asked if there was anything else about the outer part of the yard that needed attention. 'Well', said Tora, 'it's the lady with the bicycle that lives in the apartment building that never closes the gates'. Camilla said that we can't do anything about that, and Carolina replied: 'No, we just have to be extra observant. Okay, then the meeting is finished'.

The action plan to organize the schoolyard ensured that the teachers meet to try to figure out what they could do. It reminded Nils that he should draw up a map showing where to put what in the storage house, and it had motivated them to look in the boxes and do inventory, fix the lid on one of the boxes, and start making labels for the boxes. The meeting also allowed them to make plans on the fly, to ascertain that the runners' vests could be found in one spot, though this was not the intent of Lean. Still, they knew from experience that the organization of toys in the yard was a constant mess because they needed to hurry when they were closing the yard. Or, if the children were helping to tidy the yard as part of pedagogy, they didn't always follow instructions about what went where. It points to the elusive promise of plans (Abram and Weszkalnys 2013) – hoping for order that has no real possibility of being realized.

## Trying to turn Lean plans into action III

Management models do present the opportunity to talk about ways of organizing work. Whether the model's implementation works or not, the staff often finds it to be a positive experience just to discuss ways of organizing work. It can be productive if the participants can ignore some of the tools and techniques of Lean meetings in the name of Lean *improvement-group* meetings. You may remember from Chapter 3 that the municipal development strategist had recommended that Birch Preschool Unit keep the weekly preschool meetings and add a Lean-style meeting. Elm Preschool Unit opted for Lean tools and Lean-style meetings, but Birch Preschool Unit eventually decided to improve their preschool information boards. Their staff intended to create a Lean board that worked for them, which meant that they did not, in fact, create a Lean board, but made an improvement to the preschool information board.

It was the autumn of 2012, and Unit Head Christina, Pedagogist Lovisa, the four preschool heads, and two deputy preschool heads[2] met with Lean Coach Agnes (a preschool teacher) and Lean Coach Julia (an administrator in the municipality). The Lean coaches were brought in to help improve the preschool information board and turn it into a Lean board. Lean Coach Julia started by asking Christina: 'I'm a bit unsure if you want to do an *improvement board* or a *performance management board*'. Christina replied that she didn't want to get stuck in such a discussion, but instead wanted to find a board that suited their needs. Christina suggested that we should divide into two groups to discuss what they wanted the board to do for them.

After some discussion on who should be in which group, I followed the group that included Unit Head Christina, Cricket Preschool Head Nina, Bumblebee Deputy Preschool Head Karla, and Spider Preschool Head Michael. Karla started by saying that their board had names and days (see Table 3.1, Chapter 3), and that they might write for Monday, for example: 'Karla is out sick'. Karla continued:

> Today it says that Sigrid and Karla have a management group meeting. But it is a bit messy in some places. And some have a full plate, while others have nothing [no responsibilities]. But it's only about how we *arrange the day* if someone is out sick, for example. It's not an improvement board [referring to Lean].

---

2 Deputy Preschool Heads were used when the preschool head was not able to work full-time.

Arranging the day is a continuous process in preschools: every week in front of the preschool board and then again every day when the staff member responsible for arranging the day goes through the list of those who have called in sick and tries to ensure that there are enough staff members in every unit. At any one time, at least one staff member was usually sick or absent for training or meetings. Arranging the day was a frustrating task, because substitutes needed to be called in, staff moved from one unit to another, and children sometimes had to be moved to another unit. Mikael agreed with Karla, and said that they had the same system:

> Sometimes it's full and it's difficult to find room on the board. Sometimes it's difficult to find places to write both [problems]: if someone is out sick and how to arrange the day. Perhaps it's possible to have a separate column for how to arrange the day?

Nina told them about her board:

> We don't have the names, but we write who is in charge of the planning, if someone is going away to a course or something, and then we write the solution. I write the whole week on the board on Monday, and then staff can look at the board before they go out to the schoolyard in the morning.

Nina showed everyone a picture:

> As you can see, under 'deadline' is written 'teamwork statement' [connected to the Preschool Unit's Operational Plan] that needs to be finished next week. Under 'to fix' we have things such as 'if the toilet needs to be repaired'. What is needed are the areas of responsibilities and who is responsible, so that it's easy to see who is responsible for what.

Mikael said that what he missed on Nina's board was the names. He continued: 'If one forgets in what contexts one was involved, then if the names are there, it's easy to see what is relevant for oneself. Then you don't have to read the whole board'. Nina didn't agree: She said: 'They should read the whole board before they go out in the schoolyard'. Mikael changed the subject and declared:

> One thing that I've brought with me from your board, Nina is to fill in the planning time, the child-free time on the board. It works well. It creates pressure [for staff] to use it and fill in when one can see who else has answered.

Christina tried to bring everyone back to formulating the ideal preschool information board: 'Are we in agreement that we need Monday, Tuesday, Wednesday, Thursday, and Friday on the board?' Nina and Karla said in unison that the days needed to be on the board, and Christina continued by inserting the names. Nina asked why they needed the names on the board, bringing them back to the earlier disagreement. Karla said that if anyone wanted to know what Nina was doing, it would be easy to find out if her name was on the board. Nina responded that 'if I'm not on the board, then I'm present with the children, as simple as that'. Mikael said that he thought it provided a better overview if the names were on the board. He continued by saying that he wanted to develop his board with a column with how to arrange the day. Karla said yes, if three staff members were out sick, then it's on the board: 'It's possible to see on the board, but there is no room for the solution'. Christina showed an example from another preschool on her smartphone; they had added extra columns such as number of children and absences. Mikael thought that it could be a good idea to have a column for the number of children present. Mikael continued:

> One problem for creating an efficient meeting is that I want to talk about the week, whereas the teachers want to know [about what's happening] later. We need to have things in the common calendar such as the Lean process that is performed tomorrow. Now, Carina, in my division, has booked an excursion because she didn't look on the board. It should also be in the common calendar.

Christina responded: 'But the board should be about the week. Is it possible to have a separate column with the heading "to consider henceforth"? Was Carina at the weekly meeting?' Mikael said she was not. Christina laughingly added that it might be an improvement to say that everyone has to read the board. 'Now it became a bit nutty, but, okay, we have three different systems – the common calendar, the division calendars, and the boards'. Christina was referring to the common calendar for the whole preschool unit, including the different *wheels of the year* often placed around the Information board, but also on as a digital calendar on their server. She was also referring to the division calendar, which was a physical device used for more long-term planning. Finally there was an information board connected to the weekly meeting, as there is information in several places and information can get lost. Karla responded: 'But it doesn't feel like a big problem. It might just have been a mistake that Carina booked the excursion'.

Christina asked what they do at the meetings. It turned out they do it differently. In Bumblebee Preschool, division representatives brought their issues to the weekly meeting to inform each other. In Cricket Preschool, they talked about deviations and routines. Christina continued to ask: 'You go through the week. What happens next?' Mikael added: 'Now we have a democratic forum that builds on democratic representation, and then the ideas are circulated for comments in the division, and then a decision can be made'. Christina reminded everyone that decisions needed to be made formally at the monthly

*APT* workplace meetings. Mikael explained that some decisions, such as when they should have Lucia,[3] have to be made sooner – that they 'can't wait until the *APT*'. Christina looked at Nina's picture of her board and asked where the areas of responsibility were. Nina admitted that they had missed that part, but that 'it needs to be included'. Christina smiled: 'Any brilliant ideas? Do we have any brilliant ideas, before we reconvene? I overheard the other group and they talked about brilliant ideas'.

We reconvened, and Lean Coaches Julia and Agnes asked each group to draw pictures of our ideal board on brown paper. Group 2, including Bumblebee Preschool Head Sigrid, Pedagogist Lovisa, Grasshopper Preschool Head Angelica, and Grasshopper Deputy Preschool Head Annika started to explain a suggestion for a new Information board. Angelica explained that they had come up with two schedules including Monday to Friday. Schedule 1 – Monday to Friday – arranged the week:

> The lower part of the board is to visualize the contexts we're involved in. Here, at the *APT*/Collaboration/Management group square, the teachers can insert Post-its if they have something to discuss at the *APT* or for us to discuss at the management-group meeting. In Schedule 2, Monday to Friday is more informative and includes things that need to be improved. In the middle, there are things that chafe and that need to be fixed.

Nina presented the Group 1 discussion and their board, but everyone agreed that Group 2's board was a good one, even the best one, and they decided to make a possible change to that board and mainstream the preschool information boards for the next management group meeting.

In the end, it turned out that they kept the Information boards they had, at least in Bumblebee Preschool (which I saw when I did fieldwork as part of the staff a year later, in 2013). Perhaps they had no time to make changes, that they decided they were happy with the boards they had, or that they discovered that Group 2's suggestion didn't work in the end. Regardless, Lean had given them time to discuss the organization of the Information board through an improvement-group meeting. They needed a board that could incorporate co-ordination planning and planning on the fly. The fact that the new board newer materialized according to plan, despite turning a Lean process into their own focusing on what they wanted, confirmed the elusive promise of long-term plans focusing on a visionary future.

---

3 Lucia is a Swedish Christmas tradition. A group of people, in this case children, dress up in white full-length gowns with lights, a wreath of glitter in their hair or a cone with stars on their head and sing Christmas songs. The preschools invite parents as part of the end-of-year celebration (also inscribed in December as part of the *Parental Collaboration Year*). Also see https://sweden.se/culture-traditions/lucia/

## Conclusion: the agentic and affective powers of plans

Lean plans are organized to establish goals that are possible to evaluate if, when implemented, when acted upon, they fulfil the desired state that was established in the A3 (or A4) document. Lean plans are initiated for the future, creating an imagined future in which plans are fulfilled and the organization works efficiently without waste. In this way, Lean plans are plans with a vision, looking towards perfection and order, producing the hope of having continuous pedagogical documentation regularly appearing on the pedagogical documentation wall or the hope of having a flawless Lean board or a perfectly ordered schoolyard. The underlying idea is that Lean produces efficiency, and efficiency saves time, leaving more time to spend with the children. In other words, Lean plans evoke affective responses, promoting hope for a better future. But they also produce a sense of failure when it is not possible to realize them in the way Lean prescribes. There are always actions never taken.

Preschool planning is mostly about co-ordination and following the municipal directives of what needs to be done each year. Co-ordination planning is done by the existing preschool information board rather than by a Lean board. When the management group at Birch Preschool Unit tried to think of a board they needed, they ended up with an improved information board ignoring the Lean-style board but using the Lean improvement-group meeting tool to give themselves an opportunity to discuss the board. Preschool staff often practice instant planning instead, because the circumstances for engaging in preschool pedagogy are always up in the air, depending on whether all staff is in place or if the child is present whose sand place has not yet been visited. There are, of course, long-term plans in preschools: how to organize the pedagogical year, for instance (see Chapter 3), involving periods of projects and periods of evaluation, but the detailed plans, like those Lean are designed for, are often made on the fly.

Preschool planning is not for the visionary future, but a future as it is being constructed. Lean makes it possible to think of an imminent future in which all problems will be solved. Even though it was not the deliberate intent of the municipality when introducing Lean, Lean became a deception (Lashaw 2008), making an improbable future believable. The attempts to implement Lean plans kept rebellion against savings and shortage of staff at arm's length, heightening teachers' tolerance for an almost constant lack of resources.

## References

Abram, Simone and Weszkalnys, Gisa (2013), *Elusive promises: Planning in the contemporary world* (Oxford, UK: Berghahn Books).

Anderson, Ben (2006), 'Becoming and being hopeful: Towards a theory of affect', *Environment and Planning D: Society and Space*, 24 (5), 733–752.

Anderson, Ben and Holden, Adam (2008), 'Affective urbanism and the event of hope', *Space and Culture*, 11 (2), 142–159.

Appadurai, Arjun (2013), *The future as cultural fact: Essays on the global condition* (London: Verso Books).
Bloch, Ernst (1959 [1986]), *The principle of hope* (Cambridge, MA: The MIT Press).
Dodd, James (2004), 'The philosophical significance of hope', *The Review of Metaphysics*, 58 (1), 117–146.
Gramsci, Antonio (1971), *Selections from the prison notebooks* (London: Lawrence and Wishart).
Harvey, David (2000), *Spaces of hope* (Edinburgh: Edinburgh University Press).
Head, Brian W. and Alford, John (2015), 'Wicked problems: Implications for public policy and management', *Administration & Society*, 47 (6), 711–739.
Kleist, Nauja and Jansen, Stef (2016), 'Introduction: Hope over time-crisis, immobility and future-making', *History and Anthropology*, 27 (4), 373–392.
Lashaw, Amanda (2008), 'The presence of hope in a movement for equitable schooling', *Space & Culture*, 11 (2), 109.
Liker, Jeffrey K. (2004), *The Toyota way: 14 management principles from the world's greatest manufacturer* (London: McGraw-Hill).
Porter, Libby (2010), *Unlearning the colonial cultures of planning* (Farnham: Ashgate).
Preschool Curriculum (2011), 'Curriculum for the Preschool Lpfö 98 revised 2010', in Skolverket (Swedish National Agency for Education) (ed.) (Stockholm).
Rittel, Horst W.J. and Webber, Melvin M. (1973), 'Dilemmas in a general theory of planning', *Policy Sciences*, 4, 155–169.
Robertson, Alexander Foster (1984), *People and the state: An anthropology of planned development* (Cambridge studies in social anthropology; Cambridge: Cambridge University Press).
Shook, John Y. (1997), 'Bringing the Toyota production system to the United States: A personal perspective', in Jeffrey K. Liker (ed.), *Becoming Lean: Inside stories of US manufacturers* (Portland, Oregon: Productivity Press), 41–69.
Weszkalnys, Gisa (2016), 'A doubtful hope: Resource affect in a future oil economy', *Journal of the Royal Anthropological Institute*, 22 (S1), 127–146.
Womack, James P., Jones, Daniel T., and Roos, Daniel (1990), *Machine that changed the world: How Lean production revolutionized the global car wars* (New York: Simon & Schuster).
Yiftachel, Oren (1998), 'Planning and social control: Exploring the dark side', *Journal of Planning Literature*, 12 (4), 395–406.

Chapter 7

# Conclusion
The utopia of efficiency

In this book, I have developed an ethnographic account of Swedish public preschools and the preschool teachers' efforts and struggles to make sense of and use the Lean management model to improve their work organization. I have shed light on the reasons why Lean was doomed to failure in preschools. I have demonstrated the frictions that the Lean model engendered when the preschool teachers attempted to integrate it into their established working practices and organization of work and the everyday activities of preschool teachers and children. I have shown how the Lean management model and what it could offer was so fundamentally inconsistent with the preschool environment that it was not possible to align, but instead was bolted on to preschool activities. In the *Model Friction* section of this paper, I summarize and examine how the staff members tried to accomplish this task.

My interest also lies in the forces at play causing a management model from the automotive industry to seem like a good idea for preschools. There is something about the promise of something new and efficient that makes management models like Lean attractive. As Peck and Theodore (2010) have noted, a model can become a model only if there is a demand side. And for demand to occur, the model must align with something, must be ideologically anointed or sanctioned, and must have the ability to affirm and extend dominant paradigms. In the *Model Utopia* and *Model Acceleration* sections of this chapter, I discuss how the allure of newness and the promise of efficiency works as a force.

I have shown how fast policy 'model power' (Peck and Theodore 2015) works, using the Lean management model. Even when the model creates these policy problems and even when it does not solve them, management models do tend to do things. As Peck and Theodore (2010) noted: 'Substantially, models perform "formatting" functions (cf. Mitchell 2002), in that they effectively crystallize not only a preferred bundle of practices and conventions, they also stitch together particular readings of policy problems with putative solutions' (p. 171). In the *Model Power* section, I summarize and develop how the Lean management model made itself felt in Swedish public preschools. The model did accomplish some things, perhaps not what Lean gurus would have wanted it to do and perhaps not what the teachers wanted, but it did make itself felt in the preschools where I did fieldwork.

I end the book with a section entitled *Model Failure*, in which I return to discuss my thesis: The 'model power' of fast-policy management models makes them difficult to fit into the practical realities of new domains. And I discuss how the tension between the easy to use and the difficult to use in management models played out in preschools, analysed in relation to the non-translatability of management models and the model form.

## Model frictions

The Lean management model's introduction to the preschool world led to frictions between what the model could accomplish and what would be useful in preschools. The rational gaze of policy models when applied in alien domains is persistently disrupted by messy realities (Peck and Theodore 2010). In the case of the preschools, it also led to frictions that emerged from the teachers' continuous attempts to use the model, even as they were having difficulties making it align with their pedagogy and childcare and work as a useful tool in their work environment.

The Lean management model came with semantic clusters of policy words about smooth-flowing performance ridding the system of waste and about continuous improvement towards greater efficiency. The semantic clusters of Lean policy words were geared towards the delivery of an efficient product or service. The Lean model was constructed to support these goals with the use of various tools.

There is a motion in Lean towards the perfect organization, with smooth-flowing routines and standards. Waste has a specific meaning in the Lean model, based upon what is considered the problem of 'not adding value' to the perceived customer. On the assembly line, it means that all movements and any waiting time that are not adding value are waste. The whole notion is based on the elimination of movements to save time. Value-stream mappings were one of the Lean tools that would make it possible to discover that waste was not adding value to the customer; it identified flow units and cycle time and guaranteed that none of the 8 wastes were holding up the flow. When waste was identified, a Lean action plan had to be written up in the form of an A3 (or A4) problem-solving document to ensure that it was eliminated and that the efficient, free-flowing desired state was fulfilled. In this way, Lean plans were established for the future, creating imagined futures in which plans are fulfilled and the organization was working efficiently, without waste. Lean plans were plans with a vision, plans that were forward-looking, plans that were looking towards perfection and order.

The Lean board meetings were another Lean tool supporting efficiency by continuous improvement and the elimination of waste. Lean meetings worked as events-that-model (Handelman 1990 [1998]), modelling for an efficient future, focusing on such issues as evaluation, time lines, and responsible employees. As an architectural construct, the Lean board's aesthetics put the board at the centre of improvement work towards efficiency and Lean board meetings at the centre of the model. To ensure that improvements were continuous, the Lean colours of green, yellow, and red were used – used with a mission to transform. The Lean colours focused on improvements, monitoring, and evaluations: The goal was represented by green, and yellow and red indicated that there was a need for processes of transformation to reach or return to green. In the car industry, yellow and red indicated waste on the assembly line – waste that was not adding value. The colours and the Lean board worked as a 'valuation device' (Hauge 2016), targeting a smooth-flowing assembly line that could only add value to the customer.

Preschools were governed by another set of policy words that were about pedagogy, education, teaching, and care. The semantic clusters of policy words in the Preschool Curriculum and the Reggio-Emilia pedagogy were geared towards teaching children about gender equality, co-operation, democratic values, human rights, non-discrimination, and respect for differences, fostering in children the characteristics of good, well-educated citizens. Preschool policy words focused on children learning though play and projects and being able to express themselves through a hundred languages (Wurm 2005). The Lean model was constructed to support goals of efficiency and to eliminate waste by continuous improvement. Preschool activities were designed to support the Curriculum and the Reggio-Emilia pedagogy, including a variety of activities involving meetings, colours, movement (not flows), and plans – albeit with a focus quite different from the goal inherent in the Lean model.

Preschool meetings were critical tools for achieving the goals of the Curriculum and the Reggio-Emilia pedagogy. Circle-time meetings centred on taking attendance by using dolls, singing songs, and voting for where to go on excursions. These meetings placed the children at the centre, focusing on democracy and ways of co-operating as a group. The teachers' meetings, such as the pedagogical reflection meetings, placed the pedagogical project at the centre, and the teachers towards the improvement of pedagogy, ensuring that the project followed the Curriculum. The preschool planning meetings had co-ordination and instant planning at the centre. In the everyday activities of preschools, plans were focused on co-ordinating activities. Long-term plans involved the guarantee that the preschool followed the municipal organizational year or the pedagogical year visualized in the so-called *årshjul* (wheels of the year) that were developed for preschool work. Preschools often practiced instant planning, because the circumstances for engaging in preschool pedagogy were always up in the air, depending on whether all staff was in place or if the child was present whose pedagogical project was planned to be the focus that day. Thus the detailed plans, like those for which Lean is designed, were often made on the fly rather than as a plan for the future.

Because colours were used differently in preschools than they were used in Lean, there was some translation involved when Lean colours entered preschools. In the preschools, colours were used to evaluate joy at work, to discover what could be improved. According to Lean logic, joyous preschool teachers would add value to children and parents. This could, of course, be true, but according to Lean logic, teachers would be joyous if structural processes and organizational routines were made more efficient, thereby making preschool work qualitative. Lean colours needed to be used for evaluation, in order to discover and encourage continuous improvement towards efficiency. And the improvements also had to be adapted to what could be put on the Lean board and formulated under its headings. Or the problem had to be written on an A3 problem-solving document that had to include a Plan, a Do, a Check, and an Act phase. In preschools, colours were used to educate and entice play. Preschool pedagogy consisted of teaching the children about colour as one of the hundred languages, to verify that they could express themselves through colours by painting and drawing, while keeping the process joyful and imaginative.

The tools that Lean brought were constructed in such a way that they encouraged staff members to find waste in flows and structural processes rather than looking for problems in pedagogy and childcare. The same was true for what would be seen within the Lean model as waste. In preschool, there was no waste in movements in the preschools and no waiting in interaction with the children. All occasions could be made, even should be made, into pedagogical moments. Waste in the form of milk cartons or toilet rolls were made into pedagogical material as a way for children to express themselves through one of the hundred languages. Even 'real' waste became a pedagogical moment when walking to the nearby recycling station.

Apart from the contrast in policy words governing preschools and the policy words of the Lean model, Lean and preschool pedagogy worked in different spatial and temporal dimensions. Lean is about the perfectly ordered organization that will appear in the future. There is an end goal, in which continuous improvement will make the organization into a Lean organization. It is a visionary future, set *within* the spatial boundaries of the organization and making it efficient. Preschools and the Preschool Curriculum work as a model for the future, turning children into well educated, democratic, co-operative citizens, prepared for school and work. It is for a future *outside* the boundaries of preschools that preschools attempt to shape children into preferred citizens, according to the ideals of the Curriculum. The fact that Lean's future goal is placed within the organization and the preschool's future is placed outside the organization affects how they work in the present.

In the present, the Lean management model works as a socially produced smoothing machine (Bogard 2000) at many levels, smoothing the surfaces between flow units on the assembly line, cycle time in the workstations, ideas and tools, tools and work processes, and the work processes themselves. The goal of the Lean smoothing machine is to find and polish the breaks, so that waste is turned into shiny surfaces, blending in. It is the physical space of the organization, the social relations and the structures that are the focus of Lean's smoothing machine in the present. Lean is used in the present to transform the organization into a perfectly ordered, smooth-flowing organization for the future. For teachers, it is the children's wellbeing, their education, and their ways of behaving towards each other that are the present focus. Focus is not on smooth-flowing efficient structures and routines; the focus is to ascertain that the children under their care are equipped for school – and in the long run, for life – outside of preschools. According to Lean logic, children are just like cars, but instead of economic value added to a car by having a quick and efficient assembly line, children should be transformed into well educated, democratic, co-operative citizens as a way of readying them for adulthood and turning them into good citizens. In this environment, breaks and frictions present no threat, because it is not the smooth-flowing organization or the economic value of the child that is at focus. There is no need to smooth all the surfaces to make flows more efficient. In the end, there was no smoothing machine that could align and smooth between Lean and preschool care and pedagogy.

## Model utopia

Management models like Lean have a utopian dimension, in that they aspire to create the perfect organization, where everything runs smoothly in the name of efficiency. They reflect Thomas More's (1516 [2017]) *Utopia*, in that there is nothing that distracts or distorts, no pointless tasks; the people involved apply themselves and work diligently. There is no wasted time, no idleness, and no openings for depravation. It is a society that is just, ordered, stable, and secure. 'Utopias, then, are blueprints of the good (or even perfect) society, imagined elsewhere and intended as prescriptions for the near future. They are intrinsically linked to the concerns and assumptions of modernity' (Levitas 2003: 3). Management models, just like ideas about utopia, build on programmes of change and visions for an alternate world – or in this case, an alternate organization – perfectly organized, modern, and smooth flowing, without friction. Their goal is a perfect future.

Bauman (2003: 12) has noted that ideas about utopia are conditioned by modernity and modern ideas about 'territoriality' and 'finality' and contends that utopian thought took the territory for granted. It was assumed that Utopia had a ruler and that only those who belong to the place should be allowed to live there. It was the time of nation building and state building. Utopian thinking focused on the right and proper place for those who had the right to occupy this proper place, mapping and plotting the utopian map upon a particular physical territory. The good society was working as an exercise of inclusion and exclusion (Bauman 2003). Harvey (2000: 160) discusses this in terms of 'utopias as a spatial form', as a space elsewhere: in More's *island of nowhere* or urban utopias like Le Corbusier's Stockholm.

Bauman also made a point about the 'finality' of utopian thinking. The modern notion of development, of a better future, spurs on the quest for improvement, but after a series of improvements there will be a perfect society, a 'society in which any further change could be only a change to the worse' (Bauman 2003: 15). Harvey (2000) writes about the 'utopias of process' and highlights Hegel and Marx as examples. Whereas Bauman emphasizes the dark side of utopian thinking, which gave rise to Nazism and Stalinism, Harvey wanted to build a 'dialectical utopianism' as a way of creating spaces of hope for a just society, by returning to utopian movements. Bauman (2003) argues that because of the modern roots of utopian thinking, grounded as it is in territory and finality, it is difficult to align with a postmodern world. As Kumar (2003: 74) writes: 'Can there be a postmodernist utopia? Can one portray the good society in the terms of irony, scepticism, playfulness, depthlessness, ahistoricity, loss of faith in the future?'

It is, of course, true that territorially confined powers in the form of the sovereign nation state have lost some of the possibility of managing a stable order in the nation state – perhaps not as much of deterritorialization or flowing 'scapes' (Appadurai 1996) as postmodern thinking has introduced, but there is evidence that global elites are affecting global policy in ways that would have been unthinkable in the early 20th century (cf. Garsten and Sörbom 2018). The notion of the good society as the idea of searching for or developing a *perfect* society has also lost some of its appeal. Preschool teachers and the Preschool Curriculum may contribute to the good society by teaching co-operation and democracy, but they are not envisioning and striving for a perfect society – whatever that may be. But that is not the case for organizations. Ideas about the territory and finality are alive and well in the organization. It is another type of territory, comprising a physical space of social relations, where those who are included are changed on a regular basis. In this territory, the modern, utopian project of development and improvement into perfection is in good shape, not least as demonstrated by the success of management models. Management models are visionary. They are always about the future creating hope for a better workplace and better functioning work processes, but never really taking responsibility for implementation or the possibility of realizing the vision, the better future. In this way, Lean was initiated in order to create a future – to create an imagined future of a Lean, perfectly ordered organization, working efficiently without waste. The organization, in other words, has never left modernity.

## Model acceleration

Speed is the motor for modernity. As Rosa (2013) has established, we live in an 'acceleration society', which he discusses in terms of the 'escalatory logic of modernity' (Rosa 2017). It is this push for compressing time that makes room for 'fast-policy' (Peck and Theodore 2015) as represented here by the Lean management model. Policy time is speeding up and policy models circulate with increased velocity (Peck and Theodore 2010). Processing speed in computers increases continuously, the average time of sleeping and eating in Western societies is decreasing, changes in partners and residences occur more rapidly, and fashion and production cycles are shorter and shorter (Rosa 2013). Rosa's hypothesis is that modernization constitutes structural transformations of time structures and time horizons, resulting in accelerative forces.

The accelerative force is explained by Rosa's (2013) notion of 'social acceleration' and his new theory of modernity in the era of late modernity or high modernity. He reminds us that modernity requires systematic growth, innovation, and acceleration, and because time cannot be augmented or increased – only compressed (Rosa 2017) – it makes room for fast policy. Social acceleration is key to understanding modernity and the modernization process in Western societies (Rosa 2013). Rosa wants to decipher the logic of acceleration.

Rosa has argued that social acceleration is occurring in three domains. (1) *Technological acceleration* is determined by the notion that time is money and that time must be saved. It has an economic motor that points towards intentional and goal-oriented processes *within* society and is related to the industrial revolution – to what Virilio (1977 [2006]) has called the 'dromological revolution'. (2) *The acceleration of social change*, with its increase of professional specialization and division of labour has created a functional division between family and work and a changeover in jobs, partners, and political party preferences. It has a social-structural motor, which temporalizes complexity. It is not inherently goal directed, but points to accelerations *of* society itself. (3) An *acceleration of the pace of life* is the idea that there are infinite possibilities and that we should try to accomplish at much as possible as individuals. It encompasses such phenomena as speed dating, fast food, power naps, and multitasking, all of which are reactions to a perceived scarcity of time, requiring an increase in episodes of actions and experiences per unit of time. As Rosa (2013) puts it, 'the experience of an acceleration of the pace of life in modernity encompasses both an increase of the *speed of action* and a structurally induced alteration of the *experience of time* in everyday life' (p. 80).

These three domains create *the circle of acceleration*, the elements of which connect and enforce each other. Technological acceleration cannot by itself heighten the pace of life because the escalation of production could, in fact, lead to more free time. There were enormous gains in time through technological acceleration in the 20th century, as exemplified by washing machines and microwave ovens, but there is still a heightening of the pace of life, a temporal scarcity in modernity. There is structural and cultural linkage between technological acceleration and an increase in the pace of life. The circle of acceleration contracts the present; the past more quickly becomes the past and the future arrives more quickly, creating the need to rewrite the past and the present in ever shorter intervals (Rosa 2013: 77). The acceleration of social change connects by increasing the rate of decay in life and technology, and the present contracts (Rosa 2013: 77).

In such a world, there is a need for speed, for fast policy – fast policy that comes in the form of a model, moving fast and immutable, advocating efficiency, and creating the *perfect* organization.

## Model power

The utopian dimension, the ability to move quickly, makes management models a force. Management models are promoted as models for all organizations, neatly packaged into a template. The model is sold with ideas and tools linking places and professions from Senegal to Sweden, from factory workers to physicians to preschool teachers, connecting the Japan of the 1970s with the Sweden of the 2010s, yet staying basically the same. In this way, the Lean model exercises power across geographical space and historical time, allowing a moveable centre, an elusive modernity, to 'act at a distance' (Latour 1986). Even though the Lean model failed to turn the preschools into the well-oiled Lean machines it had had promised to do, it did manage to create new environments of power and new patterns of governance in preschools. The preschool teachers were set to enact efficiency according to Lean, in order to create qualitative and joyous preschools. Lean encouraged them to think of preschool activities as structural processes in need of waste elimination in order to save time.

The Lean focus on a perfect future organization working within the boundaries of preschools projected an atmosphere, a policy environment, that placed efficiency at the centre. Lean board meetings in preschools made teachers into improvement-oriented employees who focused on structure and routine in order to save time. Lean meetings concentrated not only on a particular issue, but served as a force, turning the meeting into a package, with the power to change direction. In this policy environment, colours, flow, waste, and plans were turned into something that would have been outside the preschool staff's understanding of these factors.

The Lean colours intervened in the organizational practices of the preschools by turning the focus towards evaluation and transformation, altering organizational conduct, practice, and form towards elimination of waste in the interest of saving time. The preschool teachers stood in front of Lean boards, set to evaluate their day in colours, or they participated in monitoring exercises in relation to what they had promised to do in their action plans. In this way, the colours represented a specific way of organizing work and disrupted earlier practice and conditions. The colours had agentic powers. They provoked affective responses by compelling the preschool teachers to understand green, yellow/blue, and red in relation to 'joy at work' and to connect it to the level of efficiency that would save time.

If the Lean board meeting and the Lean colours set the focus towards efficiency in a way that was not useful in preschools, the idea of investigating flows to eliminate waste through value-stream mappings were particularly unsuitable. As explained in Chapter 5, in strict Lean terms, children would be the cars on the assembly line, and the flow that would be in need of value streaming and eliminating waste was the movement of children through processes in the preschool. Or perhaps one could regard all the years children spent in the preschools as a process through which the children should flow smoothly. Fortunately, this thought never seemed to occur to the preschool teachers; instead they were forced to invent flows in which possible waste could be eliminated by organizing the schoolyard or the flow of the morning.

The Lean focus on structures and routines required the preschool teachers to invent flows and structural processes to find waste that could be eliminated to save time. Attempts to use the Lean model evoked affective responses, promoting hope for a better future: the utopia of efficiency engendered by the promise of saving time to make more time for the children. The teachers longed for this time — time that would allow them to be the educators and caregivers they wanted to be. Lean made it possible to think of an imminent future in which all their problems would be solved. Even though it was not the deliberate intent of the municipality when introducing Lean, Lean came to work as a deception (Lashaw 2008), making an improbable future believable. Attempts to implement Lean plans kept rebellion against savings and shortage of staff at arm's length, heightening teachers' tolerance for an almost constant lack of resources. And the failure of not being able to realize the plans in the way Lean prescribed was left in the hands of the preschool teachers. There were always actions that had never been taken, and actions not taken meant that the responsibility for having less time with the children fell on the shoulders of the teachers.

## Model failure

Perhaps the strangeness of introducing a management model from the automotive industry into preschools is not as strange as it is might have been perceived in the introduction of this book or when reading through the rest of the book. The utopian dreams of a smooth, efficient society and the acceleration society made room for fast policy like the Lean management model. The preschool teachers hoped that Lean efficiency would save time, and they spent many hours trying to understand the model and what it could do for them and engaging with the model by using its tools and thinking through its ideas.

Applying Lean to a preschool context was, however, doomed to failure. Its proponents failed to recognize that the context in which the Lean management model landed was fundamentally different from the context for which the model was designed. The management model form made the Lean model difficult to align with existing childcare policy, pedagogical models, and the organization of a preschool. Rather, Lean operated as a model that had been bolted on to all the preschool activities that staff was already required to handle.

Yet Lean appeared to be easy to use and made sense to implement. It was the model's power of fast, immutable mobility (Latour 1986, 1987) aligned with the perceived utopian ideal of efficiency and modernity that rushed the Lean management model into preschools as a force. Model power – its neatly packaged form, its rapid movability, its ability to affirm and extend dominant paradigms, and its template character promising improvement – comes with the promise of a solution to perceived policy problems. Management models promise something new and are designed to travel and move into new terrain, as commodities circulating and changing ownership with the help of consultants and handbooks.

There is similarity between management models and preschools, in that they operate in and are part of cultures of acceleration – a modernity that strives to improve and develop with accelerating speed. The language, ideas, technologies, and tools focus on organizational issues that could be recognized and understood as seemingly useful in most organizations – issues like continuous improvement and the elimination of waste in order to achieve efficiency. The tools of the model focus on evaluation, time lines, and responsible employees by finding a process, dividing it into flow units on the micro level, and ensuring that every waste is eliminated – all with the goal of a smooth-flowing process. There is nothing specific about these ideas and tools tying the Lean management model to the automotive industry that makes the model seem moveable. The neatly packaged model comes with tools and ideas that seem to be similar enough for it to be implemented in a preschool. This makes the model easy to use because there are elements in the model that fit pre-existing ideas of a way to make organizations efficient: goals, evaluations, continuous improvements, and action plans, for instance. And the teachers continued to try using the model in their preschools. But in practice, there are many ways in which it was difficult to use.

Even if there are some translation involved when management models travel and enter into a new organizational context, management models are possible to translate in only a minor degree and only within the framework of the model. The difficult-to-use part of the Lean management model is its dispositional difference from the policy words and tools that govern preschools. The lack of similarity between the preschool context and the context of the automobile factory renders the model inept in improving the preschool work of pedagogy and care. And it is unable to save time in the preschool environment because to do so there must be flows that can be made more efficient.

The piecemeal standardization and bureaucratization and the meticulous planning in need of a flow to find waste that was built into the Lean model did not suit preschool activities. Preschool activities are about children, not about cars and structural processes and organizational routines. Preschool activities must be continuously adapted, on the fly, in a way that Lean does not allow.

Even though Lean favours continuous improvement, it is an improvement that must be made slowly, with the intent that it be lasting, that the people involved stick to the standard in order to form the perfect organization. Preschool activities need to be continuously co-ordinated, and the practice of instant planning makes on-the-fly adaptability possible. As Scott (Scott 1998) has suggested, successful planning must include a plan for surprises and human inventiveness – the inventiveness of children and teachers. It has to favour reversibility and take small steps.

Even as a failure, Lean still managed to accomplish action and affective responses in preschools. Although it had to be bolted on to all the preschool activities that staff members already had to handle, the Lean model did suggest practices to the teachers and made certain interventions thinkable that were previously foreign to the preschool world. But this happened only as long as Lean was the go-to model for municipal activities. When my fieldwork ended in March 2014, it was not unreasonable to believe that Lean would disappear as a tool for organizing work. The municipality had just changed its municipal director and she was not a Lean advocate – albeit not actually against it. The former municipal director, who had initiated the use of the Lean management model had provided extra funding in the form of Development Strategist Gunnel for implementing Lean over a five-year period, with the intent that the model could run itself after that. This was not the case, and the Lean coaches were worried about what would happen when Gunnel had to return to her old job. After five years, the municipal director also finished her posting, and the new municipal director had no interest in continuing the extra funding. Lean is nowhere to be found in the municipal operational plan for 2018.

But what is it that I'm reading in the latest municipal operational plan? What is *närvarande ledarskap* (present leadership) – a phrase that's popping up here and there in the text? And are working conditions for preschool teachers to be improved by drawing up an action plan? Will the preschool staff again need to spend hours working on ways to improve their working conditions and discussing what *närvarande ledarskap* means? In Lean terms, it would be probably be as much of a waste of time as was the attempt to implement Lean.

If the municipality want to improve working conditions, my suggestions would be to make sure that preschool teachers have the chance to both care and educate children by adding resources in the form of more teachers per child and making sure that there are always enough teachers, regardless if staff are off sick, home with their own sick children, absent for training, or in a meeting. The new Preschool Curriculum (2011) emphasized the pedagogical responsibility preschool teachers have towards children. Teachers are not easily replaced by substitutes, especially on pedagogical assignments, because children create relationships with regular staff, which made them difficult to replace by substitutes. This was often solved by having one or two regular substitutes on call so that children would know them already, but it was still difficult to perform the pedagogical assignments if substitutes had not been part of the planning phase.

In addition, sometimes the municipal budget did not allow for employing as many substitutes as needed, which was the case when I was doing fieldwork.

Adding more teachers would help teachers feel less inadequate because they were not able to do the pedagogical project or go to the pedagogical reflection meeting planned for the week because of a lack of staff. At times this would of course mean that there might be more than enough teachers present, but not as often as policymakers might think. In any case, there are always things to do in preschools; taking extra care of the children, having time to chat and play with them, making sure that they all feel noticed and listened to. Having more teachers could also mean having the opportunity to change the pedagogical environment so that the children can experience new pedagogical challenges, or finally have the time to finish the pedagogical documentation in one go, instead of having to start, and re-start again (see Chapter 5). And if it is a question of money it might be that the money saved on not hiring consultants to explain how to use *närvarande ledarskap* or the substitutes needed when teachers are engaged in drawing up action plans for better working conditions, could at least bring a contribution towards more teachers in preschools. Regardless, this would be my suggestion.

## References

Appadurai, Arjun (1996), *Modernity at large: Cultural dimensions of globalization* (Public worlds, 99-3013247-3; 1; Minneapolis: University of Minnesota Press).

Bauman, Zygmunt (2003), 'Utopia with no Topos', *History of the Human Sciences*, 16 (1), 11–25.

Bogard, William (2000), 'Smoothing machines and the constitution of society', *Cultural Studies*, 14 (2), 269–294.

Garsten, Christina and Sörbom, Adrienne (2018), *Discreet power: How the world economic forum shapes market agendas* (Stanford: Stanford University Press).

Handelman, Don (1990 [1998]), *Models and mirrors: Towards an anthropology of public events* (Oxford, UK: Berghahn Books).

Harvey, David (2000), *Spaces of hope* (Edinburgh: Edinburgh University Press).

Hauge, Amalie Martinus (2016), 'The organizational valuation of valuation devices: Putting Lean whiteboard management to work in a hospital department', *Valuation Studies*, 4 (2), 125–151.

Kumar, Krishan (2003), 'Aspects of the Western Utopian Tradition', *History of the Human Sciences*, 16 (1), 63–77.

Lashaw, Amanda (2008), 'The presence of hope in a movement for equitable schooling', *Space & Culture*, 11 (2), 109.

Latour, Bruno (1986), 'Visualisation and cognition: Drawing things together', in Henrika Kuklick and Elizabeth Long (eds.), *Knowledge and society: Studies in the sociology of culture past and present* (6; Greenwich, CT: JAI Press).

——— (1987), *Science in action: How to follow scientists and engineers through society* (Harvard: Harvard University Press).

Levitas, Ruth (2003), 'Introduction: the elusive idea of utopia', *History of the Human Sciences*, 16 (1), 1–10.

More, Thomas (1516 [2017]), *Utopia: The Island of nowhere*, trans. Roger Clarke (Richmond: Alma Classics).
Peck, Jamie and Theodore, Nik (2010), 'Mobilizing policy: Models, methods, and mutations', *Geoforum*, 41 (2), 169–174.
—— (2015), *Fast policy: Experimental statecraft at the thresholds of neoliberalism* (Minneapolis: University of Minnesota Press).
Preschool Curriculum (2011), 'Curriculum for the Preschool Lpfö 98 revised 2010', in Skolverket (Swedish National Agency for Education) (ed.) (Stockholm).
Rosa, Hartmut (2013), *Social acceleration: A new theory of modernity* (New York: Columbia University Press).
—— (2017), 'De-synchronization, dynamic stabilization, dispositional squeeze', in Judy Wajcman and Nigel Dodd (eds.), *The sociology of speed: Digital, organizational, and social temporalities* (Oxford: Oxford University Press), 25–41.
Scott, James C. (1998), *Seeing like a state: How certain schemes to improve the human condition have failed* (Yale agrarian studies; New Haven: Yale University Press).
Virilio, Paul (1977 [2006]), *Speed and politics: An essay on dromology* (South Pasadena: Semiotext(e)).
Wurm, Julianne (2005), *Working in the Reggio way: A beginner's guide for American teachers* (St. Paul, MN: Redleaf Press).

# About the author

**Renita Thedvall** is Associate Professor in Social Anthropology. Her research is based in the field of policy and organizational anthropology, with special focus on the anthropology of bureaucracy and the state. She has a particular interest in the way policies are shaped and presented in the form of models, indicators, and standards, and how these three aspects are understood and performed. Her research projects have centred on employment policy, working life, and social issues. She has conducted field studies in the EU and Fairtrade International, and in municipal social service offices and preschools, where she has studied EU bureaucrats, standards setters, social workers' and preschool teachers' work developing, and struggling to understand, implement, and perform policies. As a part of her research, she also investigates meetings both as ethnographic objects and as sites of ethnographic inquiry. Together with Jen Sandler, she has explored this topic through an edited volume, *Meeting Ethnography: Meetings as Key Technologies of Contemporary Governance, Development and Resistance* (2017, Routledge).

# Index

acceleration 122–124, 126; the circle of 123; social 5
action plan 47, 69, 79, 91, 106, 107–109; *see also* Lean, A3 document
APT 57, 113–114
arranging the day 77, 79–80
assembly line 86–88, 91, 118, 125
audit culture 8
autonomation 25, 69

*Becoming Lean* 35

childcare policy 5–7; in comparison with England and Massachusetts 28–30, 51, 70
children in play and pedagogy 31, 34, 47–50, 69–70, 88–89, 103–104
circle-time meeting 47–50, 119; architecture 47–48, 50; maker 50, 61–62; practices of circulation 50
collaborative mode 22–23, 33, 38–39
colour 64, 119–120, 124; affective responses 68, 74, 75, 124; commodification 67; evaluation 75–78, 119; force 67, 78, 80–81; Lean 68–69, 119; medium of transformation 67–68, 75–78, 80–81; monitoring 79–80, 107–109; pedagogy 70–71; political histories 67; symbolism 66–67
continuous improvement 25, 74, 102, 118, 126
co-operation 33–34, 47–50, 119
Curriculum for the Preschool 6; *see also* Preschool Curriculum
customer pull 25
cycle time 69, 83

democratic citizens 47–50, 119

economy of words 22
efficiency 10, 27, 83, 92, 102, 115, 117, 121, 124, 125, 126
eliminating waste 25, 83–84, 86–87, 94, 98, 118, 124–125, 126
escalatory logic of modernity 84
evaluation 74, 75, 76–78, 80–81, 119
event-that models 44–45, 118
excess 85–86

failing schemes 2
failure 1, 3, 109, 115, 125; model 125–128
fast policy 2, 65, 84, 123–125
flow 25, 83, 124; efficient 84–86; smooth 84–85, 118
flow unit 69, 83, 86, 90–91, 94
friction 84, 118–121
future 61–62, 98, 100–101, 105, 115, 118, 120, 121–122, 123, 125

gender equality 30–33, 119; in comparison with Massachusetts' guidelines 32

hope 91, 98, 100–101, 115, 122

immutable mobile 2, 4, 38, 126
instruments of persuasion 22

'joy at work' 10, 64, 74–75
just-in-time production 25

language work 21, 33, 38
Lean: 5S 95; 5 Whys 86; 8 wastes 86–87, 118; 14 principles 25–27; A3 document 87, 98–99, 102, 106, 118 (*see also* action plan); automotive industry 1, 24–27, 46–47, 68–69, 86–87, 102; coach 72, 83; coach-training course 83, 89–92,

98; colours 64, 68–69, 119–120; flow 86–87; healthcare 35–36, 74–75, 87–88; improvement group meeting 46–47, 111–114; language 39; meetings 46–47, 119; monitoring 79–80, 107–109, 119; organisation in the municipality 9–10, 11–12, 37–38; policy 24–27; production 24–25; public sector 36–38; time 25, 43, 61–62, 83, 86, 91–92, 96, 119, 120; travel of 34–38; value-stream mapping 69, 86–87, 89–96; [white]board meetings 46–47, 56–61, 72–75, 118–119
*Lean Thinking* 35

*Machine that Changed the World, The* 24
makeshift ideology 7
management bureaucracy 8
management model 1, 2–8, 22, 34–38, 44–47, 117–118, 121, 124, 125
meeting ethnography 12–15, 45
meetings 43; architecture 44, 61–62; circle-time 47–50; Lean 46–47; maker 44, 61–62; management model 46–47, 119; pedagogical reflection 50–56, 119; practices of circulation 44, 61–62
method 11–15
model: acceleration 122–124; failure 17, 118, 125–128; friction 118–121; utopia 121–122
model for, model of 4
model power 3, 65, 84, 124–125, 126
modern/ity 27, 85, 101, 121–123, 124, 126; escalatory logic of 84, 122–123
monitoring 79–80, 107–109, 119
municipality, Swedish 36–37

neoliberalism 7–9
New Public Management (NPM) 8

organization 120–121, 122

PDCA (Plan, Do, Check, Act) 78, 98–99, 102, 120
pedagogical documentation 27, 50–52, 89–92, 104–105
pedagogical reflection meeting 50–56; architecture 55; maker 56; practices of circulation 55
pedagogist 54
performance 68–69
plan 98, 115, 118, 124

planning 100–101; instant 115, 119, 127; Lean 102, 106–114, 118; preschool 102–105, 119
policy: anthropology of 3; environment 38, 46, 62, 124; subjects 46; time 123
policy words 21–24, 47, 126
preschool: environment 32–33, 70; information [white]board 56–61, 111–114; Lean [white]board meeting 72–78; Lean plans into action 106–114; Lean value-stream mapping 92–96; management meeting 59–61, 111–114; organization 11–14, 31, 51, 56–58, 72–75, 92–96, 103, 106–114, 119; work 31, 34, 47–50, 50–56, 59–61, 64, 69–71, 88–89, 103–105; working conditions 9–10, 127–128
Preschool Curriculum 28–30, 31–34, 50, 105
present 61–62, 119, 120–121, 123–124

quality 10

Reggio-Emilia pedagogy 7, 28–29, 31–34, 51–52, 70–71, 119
regimes of thought 21, 34, 38

Sapir-Whorf hypothesis 66
semantic cluster 21, 38, 118–119
smooth/ing 84, 96; flows 84–85, 118, 121, 126; machines 84–86, 96, 120–121
speed 5, 122–124, 126

thing-ified 23
*This is Lean* 36
time 43, 61–62, 91–92, 121, 123, 124, 125; just-in-time 25, 86; planning 106; policy 123; stealing 83; value-added/non-value-added 86, 96
*Toyota Production System* 25
translation 3–4, 125–126

utopia 117, 121–122, 125, 126

value for the customer 25, 118, 119
value stream 25, 125
value-stream mapping 69, 86–87, 89–96, 118

waste 25, 47, 84–87, 93, 96, 118, 120, 124; elimination 83–84, 86–87, 94, 98, 124–125, 126
words 21; policy 21–24, 47, 118–120